WHO
ELIZABETH BLACKWELL:

EXCERPTS AND SPEECHES
FOR AND BY
THIS REMARKABLE WOMAN

By

VARIOUS

Read & Co.

Copyright © 2021 Brilliant Women

This edition is published by Brilliant Women,
an imprint of Read & Co.

This book is copyright and may not be reproduced or copied in any
way without the express permission of the publisher in writing.

British Library Cataloguing-in-Publication Data
A catalogue record for this book is available
from the British Library.

Read & Co. is part of Read Books Ltd.
For more information visit
www.readandcobooks.co.uk

CONTENTS

EXCERPTS DEDICATED TO ELIZABETH BLACKWELL

SPEECHES AND ESSAYS BY ELIZABETH BLACKWELL

EXCERPTS

DEDICATED TO ELIZABETH BLACKWELL

ELIZABETH BLACKWELL

By Frances E. Willard and Mary A. Livermore

Physician and author, born in Bristol, England, 3rd February. 1821. Her father, Samuel Blackwell, was a wealthy sugar refiner, a man of broad views and strong benevolence.

At the political crisis of 1830-31 commercial affairs in England were thrown into confusion, and Mr. Blackwell was among those whose fortunes were swept away at that time. He removed with his family to the United States in August. 1832, and settled in New York, where he started a sugar refinery. He was rapidly amassing wealth when the financial crash of 1837 in the United States swept away his fortune through the wreckage of the weaker houses with which he had business relations. He turned his eyes to the West, and in 1838 removed his family to Cincinnati, Ohio. There he was stricken by fever and died at the age of forty-five years, leaving a family of nine children to their own resources among strangers.

Every cent of indebtedness left by the father was paid by his children. The three older daughters, of whom Elizabeth was the third, placed themselves at once at the head of the family. Two sons in school left their studies and took clerkships. The four younger ones were still in the nursery. The older sisters opened a boarding school for young women, and their liberal culture and enterprise won them a large patronage. The sisters felt the restrictions placed upon women in th« matter of earning a livelihood, and they became convinced that the enlargement of opportunities for women was the one essential condition of their well-being in every way.

After six years of hard work, when all the younger members of the family had been placed in positions to support themselves, the sisters gave up the school.

Elizabeth resolved to study medicine, although she had to overcome a natural aversion to sickness of all kinds. She wrote to six different physicians for advice, and all agreed that it was impossible for a woman to get a medical education. She thought differently, however, and in 1844 she took charge of a Kentucky school to earn money for her expenses. In 1845 she went to Charleston, S. C., to teach music in a boarding-school, and there added a good knowledge of Latin to her French and German. There she entered the office-student class of Dr. Samuel Henry Dickson. In May, 1847, she applied for admission to the Philadelphia Medical School, but both college and hospital were closed to her. She applied to all the medical schools in the United States, and twelve of them rejected her application and rebuked her for temerity and indelicacy. The college faculty in Geneva, N. Y., and that in Castleton, Vt., considered her application, and the students in Geneva decided to favor her admission. In 1847 she entered the college as No. 417 on the register.

In January, 1849, she was graduated with the Geneva class. A large audience witnessed the granting of the first medical diploma to a woman. Immediately after graduation. Dr. Elizabeth Blackwell went to Paris, France, where, after months of delay, she was admitted to the great lying-in hospital of the Maternity as a resident pupil, and several other schools permitted her to visit. She also studied under able private tutors. In 1850 and 1851 she "walked" St. Bartholomew's hospital in London, England, studying in the Women's Hospital and under private teachers. She returned to the United States, and in the autumn of 1881 she opened an office in New York City. She succeeded in building up a large practice, in spite of social and professional antagonism and ostracism.

The Society of Friends were the first to receive her warmly and support the new movement, and she soon became known as.a reliable physician. In 1853, with her sister, Dr. Emily Blackwell, she established in New York the New York Infirmary for Women and Children, which was incoqxirated and was for some years the only woman's hospital. In 1858 and 1859 she visited England and lectured in London, Birmingham and Liverpool on the connection of women with medicine.

In 1859 she was placed on the register of English physicians. Returning to America, she entered with the warmest interest into the questions of the Civil War, and the sisters organized in the parlors of the Infirmary the Ladies' Central Relief Association, sending off the first supplies to the wounded. That association was soon merged in the Sanitary Commission, in which the sisters continued to take an active part. In 1869 Dr. Elizabeth lectured in the Medical College of the New York Infirmary, which had been chartered as a college in 1865 At the close of 1869 she went to England and settled in London, where she practiced for some years. There she founded the National Health Society and worked in a number of social reforms. She aided in organizing the London School of Medicine for Women, in which she served as the first lecturer on the diseases of women. In 1878, after a serious illness, she settled in Hastings, England, continuing her consultation practice only and working energetically for the repeal of the unjust Contagious Diseases Acts.

Up to the present time she has continued to work actively for the promotion of equal standards of morality for men and women. Of late she has become an active opponent of vivisection, regarding it as an intellectual fallacy, misleading research and producing moral injury. She gives close attention to municipal affairs, as she feels the responsibility involved in the possession of a vote, which she possesses as a householder of Hastings. She knows in advanced age no diminution of her zeal for right over wrong. In addition to her long and arduous labors as a teacher, as a student and as the pioneer woman physician. Dr. Elizabeth Blackwell has been a prolific author. Naturally, her works lie in the field of her profession. Between 1852 and 1891 she wrote the following important medical and scientific works: *The Laws of Life in Relation to the Physical Education of Girls, How to Keep a Household in Health, The Moral Education of the Young in Relation to Sex, Wrong and Right Methods of Dealing with the Social Evil, Christian Socialism, The Human Element in Sex, The Corruption of New Malthusianism, The Purchase of Women a Great Economic Blunder, The Decay of Municipal Representative Government, The Influence of Women in the Medical Profession, Erroneous Methods in Medical Education,* and *Lessons Taught by the International Hygenic Conference.* Besides these are to be counted her numerous lectures, addresses and pamphlets on many branches of her profession.

She is a woman of Unbending will and a courage that never recognized defeat as possible. She opened the gate to the medical profession for women in the United States, in France and in Great Britain, and she has lived to see that profession made as easily accessible to women as to men. Dr. Blackwell is a profound thinker, a clear and logical reasoner, and a scientific controversialist of eminent ability. Her career, her achievements, her literary and scientific productions, and her work as a practicing physician make her a standing refutation of the easygoing assumption that women have neither the endurance, nor the intellect, nor the judgment, nor the requisites to serve in the medical profession. She owns a house in Hastings, England, where she resides, with an office in London for occasional work.

A BIOGRAPHY FROM
Woman of the Century, 1893

ELIZABETH BLACKWELL

By Charlotte Fell Smith

The first woman doctor of medicine, born at Counterslip, Bristol, on 3 Feb. 1821, was third daughter of Samuel Blackwell, a Bristol sugar refiner. The father, a well-to-do Independent, emigrated with seven children in August 1832 to New York. Here Elizabeth and her sisters continued their education and became intimate with William Lloyd Garrison and other anti-slavery friends.

When Elizabeth was seventeen they removed to Cincinnati, where her father died suddenly, leaving his family of nine unprovided for. In order to support their mother and younger brothers, Elizabeth and her two sisters started a day and boarding school. They joined the Church of England, and became enthusiastic politicians and keen supporters of the movement for a wider education of women.

They were intimate with Dr. Charming and studied the writings of Emerson, Fourier, and Carlyle. In 1842 the school was relinquished. Elizabeth became head of a girls' school in Western Kentucky, which she left after a term owing to her dislike of slavery. Resolving to become a doctor in spite of the discouragement of friends, she studied medicine privately while continuing to teach in North Carolina and in Charleston. After three years she vainly applied for admission to medical schools at Philadelphia and in New York. In October 1847 she formally applied for entry to the medical class at a small university town, Geneva, in Western New York State. The entire class, on the invitation of the faculty, unanimously resolved that 'every

11

branch of scientific education should be open to all.' Outside her class she was regarded as 'either mad or bad.' She refused to assent, save by the wish of the class, to the professor's request to absent herself from a particular dissection or demonstration. No further obstacle was offered to her pursuit of the medical course. She graduated M.D. (as 'Domina' at Geneva, N.Y.) in January 1849, the first woman to be admitted to the degree (cf. gratulatory verses to 'Doctrix Blackwell,' 'An M.D. in a Gown,' in *Punch* (1849), xvi. 226).

In the following April she came to England, was courteously received by the profession on the whole, and shown over hospitals in Birmingham and London. In May, with 'a very slender purse and few introductions of value,' she reached Paris, and on 30 June entered La Maternite, a school for midwives, determined to become an obstetrician. After six months' hard work she contracted purulent ophthalmia from a patient and lost the sight of one eye. Thus obliged to abandon her hope of becoming a surgeon, she, on returning to London, obtained (through her cousin, Kenyon Blackwell) from James (afterwards Sir James) Paget, dean of St. Bartholomew's Hospital, permission to study there. She was admitted to every department except that of women's and children's diseases, and received the congratulations of Mrs. Jameson, Lady (Noel) Byron, Miss Rayner (Mdme. Belloc), Miss Leigh Smith (Madame Bodichon), the Herschells, Faraday, and Florence Nightingale.

Meanwhile her sister Emily was studying for a doctor at Cleveland, Ohio, and in 1854 acted as assistant to Sir James Simpson in Edinburgh, but declined an urgent request to go to the Crimea.

Elizabeth went back to America in 1850, and was refused the post of physician to the women's department of a dispensary in New York. She spent her leisure in preparing some excellent lectures on the physical education of girls ('Laws of Life,' New York, 1852). In 1853 she opened a dispensary of her own, which was incorporated in 1854 as an institution of women physicians for the poor, and developed into the New York Infirmary and College for Women. Joined in 1856 by her sister Emily, who had now also qualified at Cleveland, and by Marie Zackrzewska (a Cleveland student in whose education she had taken much interest and the third woman to qualify), she opened in New York in May 1857 a hospital entirely conducted by women. Opposition was great, but the quakers of New York gave valuable support from the first. In 1858 Elizabeth revisited England and gave lectures at the Marylebone Literary Institution on the value of physiological and medical knowledge to women and on the medical work already done in America. Liverpool, Manchester, and Birmingham welcomed her, and she issued an English edition of 'Laws of Life' (1859; 3rd edit. 1871). A proposal was made to establish a hospital for women's diseases, to which the Comtesse de Noailles, the Hon. Russell Gurney, and others contributed handsomely. Dr. Elizabeth Blackwell's name was placed upon the British medical register on 1 Jan. 1859, ten years after she had qualified.

Again in America, Elizabeth joined her sister in a rapidly growing hospital practice. Students came to them from Philadelphia. At the outbreak of the American civil war they established the Ladies Sanitary Aid Institute and the National Sanitary Aid Association, and organised a plan for selecting, and training for the field, nurses whose services did much to win sympathy for the entire movement. In 1865 the trustees of the infirmary obtained a charter. The Blackwells would have preferred to secure the benefits of joint medical instruction, but, failing this, they organised a full course of college instruction, with hygiene as one of the principal chairs, an independent examination board, and a four years course of study. Elizabeth delivered the opening address on 2 Nov. 1868, and held the first professorship of hygiene. Dr Sophia Jex-Blake (*d.* 1912) was among her first students. In twenty years free and equal entrance of women into the profession of medicine was secured in America.

Elizabeth returned to England with a view to the same end. She settled in Jurwood Place, Marylebone, where in 1871, a drawing-room meeting, the National Health Society was formed. She lectured the Working Women's College on 'How to keep a Household in Health' (published 1870), and on 'The Religion of Health' 3rd edit. 1889) to the Sunday Lecture Society, but in 1873 her health gave way and she travelled abroad. At the London School of Medicine for Women, opened in 1875, she accepted the chair of gynaecology, he took an active part in the agitation against the Contagious Diseases Act. During a winter at Bordighera she wrote 'The Moral Education of the Young considered under Medical and Social Aspects,' which under its original title, Counsel to Parents on the Moral Education of their Children,' was refused by twelve publishers, and at last appeared through the intervention of Jane Ellice Hopkins (2nd edit. 1879). She also contributed an article on 'Medicine and Morality' to the 'Modern Review' (1881). Miss Blackwell delivered the opening address at the London School of Medicine for Women in October 1889, and revisited America in 1906; but an accident in Scotland enfeebled her in 1907, and she died at her home, Rock House, Hastings, on 31 May 1910, in her ninetieth year. She was buried at Kilmun, Argyll. A portrait from a sketch by the Comtesse de Charnacee, Paris, 1859, hangs at the London School of Medicine for Women.

A BIOGRAPHY FROM
Dictionary of National Biography, 1912 supplement, Volume 1

ELIZABETH BLACKWELL

By Alfreda B. Withington

Elizabeth Blackwell, the first woman to receive a medical degree, was born in Bristol, England, February 3, 1821, the daughter of Samuel Blackwell, a sugar refiner of progressive ideas and prepossessed in favor of American institutions. In 1832 he settled in New York with his family, and being the only man in America who then understood the process of refining sugar by the use of vacuum plans, he was in a fair way to make a fortune. But his refinery was burned, and in 1838 he moved to Cincinnati, partly with the hope of introducing the cultivation of beet sugar, and thereby dealing a severe blow at slavery by making the slave-grown cane-sugar unprofitaable. But he died soon after, leaving his family dependent upon their own exertions. The mother and the three oldest daughters opened a school and Elizabeth's uncommon strength of character showed itself in her good discipline. The family continued their anti-slavery work and threw themselves ardently into the movement for the higher education of women.

When the brothers were old enough to go into business the school was given up, and Elizabeth went to Henderson, Kentucky, to teach a district school. She astonished the southern ladies by her courage in taking long walks through the woods when they were afraid of negroes and the savage dogs which abounded.

She was led to turn her attention to medicine through the severe illness of a woman friend. Medicine in itself was not attractive, but she believed there was need of women physicians.

She wrote to several physicians about her plan and their replies were that the idea was good, but impossible. In 1845 she went to teach at Asheville, Nova Scotia, in the school kept by the Rev. John Dickson, who had previously been a doctor. Here she studied medicine privately, earning money by teaching. In 1847 she went to Philadelphia, studied anatomy under Dr. Allen, and applied for admission to each of the four medical colleges of that city, but in vain.

Applications to the large medical schools of New York also proving unsuccessful, she sent requests to twelve of the country colleges. Geneva consented. The medical class there of 150 students was composed of a riotous, boisterous, and unmanageable set, who had given the faculty and town much trouble. The letter was referred to the students for decision, and the announcement was received with most uproarious demonstrations of favor and extravagant speeches. The faculty received the vote of approval with evident disfavor, but admitted the woman student. On Miss Blackwell's appearance in the lecture-rooms some weeks later the class was transformed by magic into an orderly body of students, and this continued throughout the term. Professors and students showed her every courtesy, and she was never molested after a few unsuccessful practical jokes. The outside public, however, greatly disapproved of her, and she was considered by them to be either a bad woman or insane.

She graduated in 1849. The event caused a considerable stir in England as well as in America, and *Punch* gave her some complimentary verses. In London and Paris where she next studied Dr. Blackwell made many valued friends including Lady Byron and Florence Nightingale. While a resident at La Maternité in Paris, Dr. Blackwell had the misfortune to contract a purulent ophthalmia, which cost her six months illness and the sight of one eye. In 1851 she returned to America and began practice in New York with her sister Emily who had gained her medical diploma in 1854 at the Cleveland Medical College. But it was still considered highly scandalous for a woman to be a doctor. Patients came slowly and socially she was ostracized. She even had difficulty in renting a respectable consulting-room. One landlady who sympathized with her lost all her other lodgers by taking her in and Elizabeth finally had to buy a house with borrowed money. The first time she called in consultation a man physician—a man eminent in the profession—he walked about the room exclaiming it was an extraordinary case, that he was in great difficulty; at first she was puzzled, for though the case of illness was severe, it was not unusual. At last she comprehended that he referred not to the patient but to the situation: could he without loss of professional dignity act as a consultant to a woman physician. He finally decided he could and became a firm friend of the woman physicians.

Not being allowed to practise in the existing dispensaries, she started a little one of her own in 1857, and, with her sister, Emily, and Dr. Marie Zakrzewska, founded the New York Infirmary for Women and Children. This was the first hospital conducted wholly by women, and met with strong opposition.

When the Civil War broke out Dr. Blackwell called a meeting to discuss the providing of trained nurses, and from this meeting grew the National Sanitary Aid Association. She also anticipated modern developments by organizing the services of sanitary visitors in the slums of New York.

In 1865 when the Woman's Medical College of New York Infirmary was founded, Dr. Blackwell occupied the chair of hygiene. When Cornell opened its medical department, the college was merged with that at Cornell.

After having established the New York Infirmary and College, feeling that perhaps she could do more for the cause in England she returned there in 1869. She took a house and began practice in London where she identified herself with the Medical Woman Movement, Woman's Suffrage and with Mrs. Josephine E. Butler in her seventeen years' war against state regulation of vice. In a short time her health failed, she could not stand the London climate, she traveled on the continent for a year or two and they bought a house at Hastings, living there until her death May 31, 1910, at the age of eighty-nine.

During her life at Hastings she kept up her London connections and interests and by her pen aided the movements in which she was interested.

Her most important book was "Counsel to Parents on the Moral Education of Children," 1876, which has been translated into French and German.

Other important writings were: "The Laws of Life," 1852; "Medicine as a Profession for Women," 1860; "The Religion of Health," 1869; "Wrong and Right Methods of Dealing with the Social Evil," 1883; "The Human Element in Sex," 1884; "Pioneer Work in Opening the Medical Profession to Women," 1895.

A BIOGRAPHY FROM
American Medical Biographies, 1920

OBITUARY OF
ELIZABETH BLACKWELL

1910

ELIZABETH BLACKWELL, M.D.,
CONSULTING PHYSICIAN,
NEW HOSPITAL FOR WOMEN.

Dr. Elizabeth Blackwell died at Hastings on May 31st, in her ninetieth year, after a long illness, which would seem to have originated in a fall while on a visit to Scotland in 1907.

She was the first woman to be admitted to the British *Medical Register*, and her success is the more notable in that, apart from difficulties brought about by the total novelty of the idea of a woman studying medicine, she had to contend with one experienced by many male students, namely, lack of means. She was the daughter of a Bristol sugar refiner, who, emigrating to the United States in 1832, died a few years later, leaving hardly any fortune behind him and a family of nine children, headed by three girls, of whom Elizabeth Blackwell, then aged 17, was the youngest. To keep the family going this trio opened a small school, carrying it on successfully for four years, until a brother was old enough to begin a business life. Elizabeth Blackwell was then persuaded, somewhat against her will, to see if medicine did not offer her a career, and finally was accepted as a pupil at the medical school carried on at Geneva University in the State of New York. She was admitted to the school as the result of a vote among its students, who, from beginning to end, treated her with admirable courtesy. On one occasion the anatomy teacher warned her to absent herself during a particular dissection, but she replied that she was a student, and a student only, and would attend it, unless her fellow-students wished her not to do so. The result was that she took her place as usual, her fellow-students carefully abstaining from any kind of conduct which might possibly accentuate the awkwardness of the situation. On leaving this school with the degree of M.D. in 1849, she spent two years in Europe, dividing her time between St. Bartholomew's, where she was welcomed by the then dean of the school, the late Sir James Paget, and the Maternity Hospital at Paris. While at the latter she had an unfortunate accident, losing the sight of one eye, which became infected while she was treating a patient with gonorrhoea. This put an end to her hopes of figuring in surgery rather than in medicine.

On returning to the United States she began to practice in partnership with one of her sisters, eventually establishing a dispensary out of which grew the New York Infirmary for Women. She also gave lectures to women on the laws of life in reference to the physical education of girls. In 1859 she paid a further visit to England, during which she lectured on medicine as a profession for women. Among one of her audiences was Miss Garrett, now Mrs. Garrett-Anderson, who shortly afterwards began, in her turn, the study of medicine, qualifying as the first woman doctor of English education in 1865. Just before her return to America it was suggested to Miss Blackwell that she should get her name inscribed in the recently instituted *Medical Register*, and but for this almost accidental circumstance she might not have spent the last forty years of her existence in this country. She only returned to it after some eight years' further work in America, during which she played an active part in the organization of women's nursing during the civil war. One outcome of this work was the establishment of a medical school for women in which Miss Blackwell, who, in her visits to England, had come under the influence of Miss Nightingale, held the Chair of Hygiene.

When she finally settled in England she continued to co-operate in the movement which has since led to the frank recognition of the medical profession as a proper sphere for women, and to the establishment, as we recently pointed out, of as many as 476 registered medical women in practice in England alone.

For a long time Dr. Blackwell carried on an active practice partly in London, partly in Hastings. Of late years she had not been seen much in London, but she was always certain to be acclaimed at the London (R. F. H.) School of Medicine for Women, where at one time she lectured on gynaecology. She also held, up to the time of her death, a position on the consulting staff of the New Hospital for Women. She was the author of a good many publications; among the more important being *The Laws of Life in Relation to the Physical Education of Girls*, *The Human Element in Sex*, *The Religion of Health*, and *The Moral Education of the Young in Relation to Sex in Medical and Social Aspects*.

There are two points never to be forgotten in speaking of Dr. Elizabeth Blackwell: one is that, although much of her life was passed in America, she did not go to that country until she was 11 years old, and always regarded herself as English. The second is that, although never married, she was, and ever remained, one of the most womanly of women. It was, indeed, her womanly character, coupled with her intense earnestness, which mainly enabled her to overcome the difficulties in her path, and won for her personally, if not for her ambitions in respect of women as a whole, the esteem and good wishes of all possible opponents. Although she appears to have turned to medicine with some reluctance in the first place, she soon acquired a belief that she had a definite "call," and retained this belief to the end.

The interment took place at Kilmun, and the funeral service

was attended by representatives of various medical and other societies connected with the work in which Dr. Blackwell took so prominent a part.

PUBLISHED IN THE
British Medical Journal, 1910

SPEECHES
AND ESSAYS

BY ELIZABETH BLACKWELL

MEDICINE AS A
PROFESSION FOR WOMEN[1]

1860

In inviting consideration to the subject of medicine as an occupation for women, it is not a simple theory that we wish to present, but the results of practical experience. For fourteen years we have been students of medicine; for eight years we have been engaged in the practice of our profession in New York; and during the last five years have, in addition, been actively occupied in the support of a medical charity. We may therefore venture to speak with some certainty on this subject; and we are supported by the earnest sympathy of large numbers of intelligent women, both in England and America, in presenting this subject for the first time to the public.

The idea of the education of women in medicine is not now an entirely new one; for some years it has been discussed by the public, institutions have been founded professing to accomplish it, and many women are already engaged in some form of medical occupation. Yet the true position of women in medicine, the real need which lies at the bottom of this movement, and the means necessary to secure its practical usefulness and success, are little known. We believe it is now time to bring this subject forward and place it in its true light, as a matter not affecting a few individuals only, but of serious importance to the community at large; and demanding such support as will allow of the establishment of an institution for the thorough education of women in medicine.

When the idea of the practice of medicine by women is suggested the grounds on which we usually find sympathy expressed for it are two. The first is, that there are certain departments of medicine in which the aid of *women* physicians would be especially valuable to women. The second argument is, that women are much in need of a wider field of occupation, and if they could successfully practice any branches of medicine it would be another opening added to the few they already possess. In some shape or other, these two points are almost universally regarded (where the matter has been considered at all) as the great reasons to be urged in its behalf.

Now, we believe that both these reasons are valid, and that experience will fully confirm them; but we believe also that there is a much deeper view of the question than this; and that the thorough education of a class of women in medicine will exert an important influence upon the life and interests of women in general, an influence of a much more extended nature than is expressed in the above views. The question of the real value to the community of what women may do in medicine is an eminently practical matter, for upon it is based the aid which they may ask for its accomplishment; and upon the position of women in medicine depends the kind and extent of education which should be given to fit them for it. A great deal of well-meant effort has been, and is still being expended upon the institutions which have been established for this purpose. Sometimes we have heard much discouragement expressed at the slight result that has followed from them; while, on the other hand, it is often said, "after all, it is a matter for women to settle for themselves, if they can be doctors, and want to, they will find the way to do it, there is no need of doing any thing in the matter." Now as I have said, we believe it to be by no means a matter concerning only the limited number of women who may be actually engaged in the pursuit itself; and it is also certain that to insure the success of the work it is not enough that women should wish to study, the coöperation and support of public sentiment is needed to enable them to do so. We hope, by showing the value of the work, to prove it to be the interest of the community to carry it out; and we desire to show the means by which this may be done.

Let me then say a few words on the influence which would be exerted on society by the opening of medicine as a profession to women. The interests and occupations of women, as they actually are at present, may be referred to four distinct forms of effort:—Domestic life; the education of youth; social intercourse, and benevolent effort of various kinds. All these avocations, by unanimous consent, are especially under the superintendence of women, and every woman, as she takes her place in society, assumes the responsibility of participation in some of them.

While these pursuits have always formed the central interest of the majority of women, their character, and the requirements which they make for their proper performance, have widened, with the advance of modern society, in a remarkable degree. Social intercourse—a very limited thing in a half civilized country, becomes in our centres of civilization a great power, establishing customs more binding than laws, imposing habits and stamping opinions, a tribunal from whose judgment there is hardly an appeal. All who are familiar with European life, and the life of our great cities, know what an organized and powerful force it ever tends to become.

In like manner, benevolent efforts have little influence in new countries, but in Europe, especially in England, the extent of such work, and the amount of it which is done by women would be incredible, did we not see here, in our midst, the commencement of a similar state of things.

Domestic life is not less affected by the growth of the age; the position and duties of the mother of a family call for very different qualifications, in the wide and complicated relations of the present, from what was needed a century ago.

Now it is evident that the performance of all these forms of work, extended and organized as they are, is in its practical nature a business requiring distinct knowledge and previous preparation, as much as actual trades and professions. This fact would be more commonly recognized were it not that there is so much moral and spiritual life interwoven into woman's work by the relations upon which it is founded, and out of which it grows, as to make it more difficult to separate this business aspect of her work from her personal life, than is the case with the business life of men; consequently its practical character is too often considered entirely subordinate, or lost sight of. Every woman, however, who brings thought and conscience to the performance of everyday duties, soon realizes it in her own experience. The wider the view she takes of life, the higher her ideal of her domestic and social relations, the more keenly she will feel the need of knowledge with regard to this matter of fact basis upon which they rest. The first and most important point in which she will feel the want of this previous training will be in her ignorance of physiological and sanitary science, in their application to practical life; of the laws of health and physical and mental development; of the connection between moral and physical conditions, and the influences which our social and domestic life exert upon us. These and similar questions will meet her at every step, from the commencement of her maternal life, when the care of young children and of her own health bring to her a thousand subjects of perplexity, to the close of her career, when her children, assuming their positions as men and women, look to her as their natural counsellor.

It may be said, at first sight, that in these things it is not so much knowledge as common sense and earnestness that is wanted; that as health is the natural condition, it will be secured by simply using our judgment in not positively disregarding what our natural instincts teach us in regard to our lives. This would be true if civilization were a simple state directed by instinct; but every advance in social progress removes us more and more from the guidance of instinct, obliging us to depend upon reason for the assurance that our habits are really agreeable to the laws of health, and compelling us to guard against the sacrifice of our physical or moral nature while pursuing the ends of civilization.

From the fact, then, that our lives must be directed more by reason than instinct, arises at once the necessity for a science of health, and that comprehension of it which will lead to its daily application. Take in illustration the simplest physical need, that which is most completely instinctive in its character—the question of food. Animals make no mistake on this point, being governed infallibly by instinct, but what conflicting theories it has given rise to among men! It is very rare to find among women, the heads of families, any clear idea of what are the requisites for a healthy table; and what is true of this very simple material want is still more so with regard to higher questions of physical law, those more intimately connected with the intellect and affections, and the family and social relations growing out of them. Nothing is more striking in a wide observation of daily life than the utter insufficiency of simple common sense to secure wise action in these matters. Numbers of people, of very good common sense in other things, violate the fundamental laws of health without knowing it; and when they think upon the subject they are just as likely to follow some crude popular theory as to find out the truth.

That progress is needed in sanitary matters is widely admitted; sanitary conventions are held; the medical profession and the press are constantly calling attention to defects of public and private hygiene, pointing out the high rate of mortality amongst children, etc.; but it is far from being as generally recognized how essential to progress it is that women, who have the domestic life of the nation in their hands, should realize their responsibility, and possess the knowledge necessary to meet it.

In education, as in domestic life, the same necessity for hygienic knowledge exists. Statistics show that nine-tenths of our teachers are women, and it is obviously a matter of great importance that they should be familiar with the nature and needs of the great body of youth which is intrusted to their care. It is not possible that our systems of education should be really suited to childhood, training its faculties without cramping or unduly stimulating the nature, unless those by whom this work is done understand the principles of health and growth upon which school training should be based. Our school education ignores, in a thousand ways, the rules of healthy development; and the results, obtained with much labor and expense, are gained very generally at the cost of physical and mental health.

If, then, it be true that health has its science as well as disease; that there are conditions essential for securing it, and that every day life should be based upon its laws; if, moreover, women, by their social position, are important agents in this practical work, the question naturally arises, how is this knowledge to be widely diffused among them? At present there exists no method of supplying this need. Physiology and all branches of science bearing upon the physical life of man are pursued almost exclusively by physicians, and from these branches of learning they deduce more or less clear ideas with regard to the conditions of health in every-day life. But it is only the most enlightened physicians who do this work for themselves; a very large proportion of the profession, who are well acquainted with the bearing of this learning upon disease, would find it a difficult matter to show its relation to the prevention of disease, and the securing of health, by its application to daily life. If this be the case with regard to physicians, it must evidently be impossible to give to the majority of women the wide scientific training that would enable them from their own knowledge to deduce practical rules of guidance. This must be done by those whose avocations require wide scientific knowledge—by physicians. Yet the medical profession is at present too far removed from the life of women; they regard these subjects from such a different stand-point that they can not supply the want. The application of scientific knowledge to women's necessities in actual life can only be done by women who possess at once the scientific learning of the physician, and as women a thorough acquaintance with women's requirements—that is, by women physicians.

That this connecting link between the science of the medical profession and the every-day life of women is needed, is proved by the fact that during the years that scientific knowledge has been accumulating in the hands of physicians, while it has revolutionized the science of medicine, it has had so little direct effect upon domestic life. Twenty years ago, as now, their opinion was strongly expressed with regard to the defects in the adaptation of modern life and education to the physical well being of society, and particularly of its injurious results to women. Yet, as far as these latter are concerned, no change has been effected. In all such points women are far more influenced by the opinions of society at large, and of their elder women friends, than by their physician, and this arises from the fact that physicians are too far removed from women's life; they can criticize but not guide it. On the other hand, it is curious to observe that, as within the last few years the attention of a considerable number of women has been turned to medicine, the first use they have made of it has been to establish a class of lecturers on physiology and hygiene for women. They are scattered all over the country; the lectures are generally as crude and unsatisfactory as the medical education out of which they have sprung; but the impulse is worthy of note, as showing the instinctive perception of women, as soon as they acquire even a slight acquaintance with these subjects, how directly they bear upon the interests of women, and the inclination which exists to attempt, at least, to apply them to their needs. As teachers, then, to diffuse among women the physiological and sanitary knowledge which they need, we find the first work for women physicians.

The next point of interest to be noticed is the connection of women with public charities and benevolent institutions.

In all civilized nations women have always taken an active share in these charities; indeed, if we include those employed in the subordinate duties of nurses, matrons, etc., the number of women actually engaged would much outnumber that of men. How large a part of the character of these institutions, and of the influence exerted by them upon society, is dependent upon this great body of women employed in them and connected with them, may readily be imagined. Yet it is certain, and admitted by all who have any acquaintance with the matter, that this influence at present is far from being a good one. It is well known how much the efficiency of women as managers or supporters of public institutions is impaired by the lack of knowledge and practical tact to second their zeal; and business men who have dealings with them in these relations are very apt to regard them as troublesome and uncertain allies, rather than as efficient coworkers. With those employed in the active care of the institutions the case is still worse; the very term hospital nurse conveys the idea of belonging to a degraded class.

How to obviate this great evil has become an important question. In England, where all public institutions, hospitals—civil and military—workhouses, houses for reformation, prisons, penitentiaries, etc., form a great system, dealing with the poorer classes to an immense extent, and having a social importance too serious to be overlooked, the question has assumed sufficient weight to be discussed earnestly by government and the public at large.

In Catholic countries this is accomplished to a certain extent—that is, as far as the domestic and nursing departments are concerned—by the religious orders, the sisters of charity and others. Every one who is familiar with such institutions must have been struck by the contrast between the continental and English hospitals, etc., caused by this one thing, by the cheerful and respectable home-like air of well-managed French establishments, as compared with the gloomy, common aspect of even wealthy English or American charities; and must have observed the salutary influence upon patients, students, and all connected with these places, of the presence and constant superintendence of women who, instead of being entirely common and subordinate, are universally regarded with respect and confidence, and by the poorer classes almost with veneration.

It is very common among both Catholics and Protestants to consider these sisterhoods as the result entirely of religious enthusiasm, and to assert that large bodies of women can only be induced to accept these occupations, and carry them out in this efficient manner from this motive. When efforts have been made in England and Germany to establish any thing of the kind among Protestants, it is always to the religious element that the appeal has been made. Many such efforts have been made, with more or less success, in Germany. In England, the results have been very imperfect, and have entirely failed to secure any thing approaching in practical efficiency to the Catholic sisterhoods.

Now these failures are very easily comprehended by any one who has seen much of these sisters in actual work, for such persons will soon perceive that the practical success of these orders does not depend upon religious enthusiasm, but upon an excellent business organization. Religious feeling there is among them, and it is an important aid in filling their ranks and keeping up their interest; but the real secret of their success is in the excellent opening afforded by them for all classes of women to a useful and respected social life. The inferior sisters are plain, decent women, nothing more, to whom the opportunity of earning a support, the companionship, protection and interest afforded by being members of a respected order, and the prospect of a certain provision for age, are the more powerful ties to the work, from the fact that they are generally without means, or very near connexions, and would find it difficult to obtain a better or so good a living. The superior sisters are usually women of character and education, who, from want of family ties, misfortune, or need of occupation, find themselves lonely or unhappy in ordinary life; and to them the church, with its usual sagacity in availing itself of all talents, opens the attractive prospect of active occupation, personal standing and authority, social respect, and the companionship of intelligent co-workers, both men and women—the feeling of belonging to the world, in fact, instead of a crippled and isolated life. For though it is common to speak of the sisters as renouncing the world, the fact is, that the members of these sisterhoods have a far more active participation in the interests of life than most of them had before. No one can fully realize the effect this has upon them, unless they have at once seen them at their work, and are aware how welcome to great numbers of women would be an active, useful life, free from pecuniary cares, offering sympathy and companionship in work and social standing to all its members, with scope for all talents, from the poorest drudge to the intelligent and educated woman—an offer so welcome as to be quite sufficient to overcome the want of attraction in the work itself at first sight.

As we have said, every effort so far to introduce a corresponding class of women into English institutions has proved a failure, for there is no such organization in external life in Protestant churches as there is in the Catholic; it is contrary to the genius of the nation; and the same results would certainly follow in America.

The only way to meet the difficulty, to give a centre to women who are interested in such efforts, and to connect intelligent women with these institutions, is to introduce women into them as physicians. If all public charities were open to well educated women physicians, they would exert upon them the same valuable influence that is secured by the presence and services of the superiors of these orders; they would bring in a more respectable class of nurses and train them, which no men can do; they would supervise the domestic arrangements, and give the higher tone of womanly influence so greatly needed.

They would be at the same time a connecting link between these establishments and women in general life, enlisting their interest and active services in their behalf, far more effectually than could be done by any other means. A real and great want would thus be supplied, and one which no other plan yet proposed has proved at all adequate to meet.

We come now to the position of women in medicine itself. The fact that more than half of ordinary medical practice lies among women and children, would seem to be, at first sight proof enough that there must be here a great deal that women could do for themselves, and that it is not a natural arrangement that in what so especially concerns themselves, they should have recourse entirely to men. Accordingly we find that, from the very earliest ages, a large class of women has always existed occupying certain departments of medical practice. Until within half a century, a recognized position was accorded to them, and midwives were as distinct a class, as doctors. Even now, in most European countries, there are government schools for their instruction, where they are most carefully trained in their own speciality. This training is always given in connexion with a hospital, of which the pupils perform the actual practice, and physicians of standing are employed as their instructors. In Paris, the great hospital of La Maternité, in which several thousand women are received annually, is entirely given up to them, and Dubois, Professor of Midwifery in the medical school of Paris, is at the head of their teachers. Until within a few years, it was common for eminent French physicians to receive intelligent midwives as their private pupils, and take much pains with their education. They were also admitted to courses of anatomical instruction in the Ecole Pratique, and an immense amount of practice was in the hands of these women. The whole idea of their education, however, planned and molded entirely by men, was not to enable these women to do all they could in medicine, but to make them a sort of supplement to the profession, taking off a great deal of laborious poor practice, and supplying a certain convenience in some branches where it was advantageous to have the assistance of skilful women's hands. With the advance of medical science, however, and its application to all these departments of medicine, this division of the directing head, and the subordinate hand, became impossible. Physicians dismissed, as far as possible, these half-educated assistants, excluded them from many opportunities of instruction under their authority, and in the government schools, which popular custom still upholds, they have materially curtailed their education. Nor is it possible or desirable to sanction the practice of any such intermediate class. The alternative is unavoidable of banishing women from medicine altogether, or giving them the education and standing of the physician. The broad field of general medical science underlies all specialities, and an acquaintance with it is indispensable for the successful pursuit of every department. If the popular instinct that called women so widely to this sort of work represent a real need, it can only be met now by a class of women whose education shall correspond to the wider requirements of our present medical science.

Moreover, experience very soon shows that it is not these special branches of practice that will chiefly call for the attention of women in medicine. The same reason which especially qualifies women to be the teachers of women, in sanitary and physiological knowledge, viz., that they can better apply it to the needs of women's life, holds good in regard to their action as physicians. So much of medical practice grows out of every-day conditions and interests, that women who are thoroughly conversant with women's lives will, if they have the character and knowledge requisite for the position, be as much better qualified in many cases to counsel women, as men would be in similar circumstances to counsel men. At present, when women need medical aid or advice, they have at once to go out of their own world, as it were; the whole atmosphere of professional life is so entirely foreign to that in which they live that there is a gap between them and the physician whom they consult, which can only be filled up by making the profession no longer an exclusively masculine one. Medicine is so broad a field, so closely interwoven with general interests, dealing as it does with all ages, sexes, and classes, and yet of so personal a character in its individual applications, that it must be regarded as one of those great departments of work in which the coöperation of men and women is needed to fulfill all its requirements. It is not only by what women will do themselves in medicine, but also by the influence which they will exert on the profession, that they will lead it to supply the needs of women as it can not otherwise.

Our own experience has fully proved to us the correctness of this view. We find the practice, both public and private, which comes naturally to us is by no means confined to any special departments, and where patients have sufficient confidence in us to consult us for one thing, they are very apt to apply in all cases where medical aid is needed. The details of our medical work during the number of years that we have been connected with the profession can not be given to the public, but they have fully satisfied us that there will be the same variety in the practice of women as exists in that of men; that individual character and qualification will determine the position in practice, rather than pre-conceived ideas with regard to the position; and that there is no department in which women physicians may not render valuable services to women.

It is often objected to this idea of professional and scientific pursuits for women that it is too much out of keeping with their general life, that it would not harmonize with their necessary avocations in domestic and social life; that the advantages to be gained from the services of women physicians would not compensate for the injurious effect it would have upon the women themselves who pursued the profession, or the tendency it might have to induce others to undervalue the importance of duties already belonging to them.

This objection, the prominent one which we usually meet, appears to us based on an entire misapprehension of what is the great want of women at the present day. All who know the world must acknowledge how far the influence of women in the home, and in society, is from what it should be. How often homes, which should be the source of moral and physical health and truth, are centers of selfishness or frivolity! How often we find women, well meaning, of good intelligence and moral power, nevertheless utterly unable to influence their homes aright. The children, after the first few years of life, pass beyond the influence of the mother. The sons have an entire life of which she knows nothing, or has only uneasy misgivings that they are not growing up with the moral truthfulness that she desires. She has not the width of view—that broad knowledge of life, which would enable her to comprehend the growth and needs of a nature and position so different from hers; and if she retain their personal affection, she can not acquire that trustful confidence which would enable her to be the guardian friend of their early manhood. Her daughters also lack that guidance which would come from broader views of life, for she can not give them a higher perception of life than she possesses herself. How is it, also, with the personal and moral goodness attributed to woman, that the tone of social intercourse, in which she takes so active a part, is so low? That, instead of being a counterpoise to the narrowing or self-seeking spirit of business life, it only adds an element of frivolity and dissipation.

The secret of this falling short from their true position is not a want of good instinct, or desire for what is right and high, but a narrowness of view, which prevents them from seeing the wide bearing of their duties, the extent of their responsibilities, and the want of the practical knowledge which would enable them to carry out a more enlightened conception of them. The more connections that are established between the life of women and the broad interests and active progress of the age, the more fully will they realize this wider view of their work. The profession of medicine which, in its practical details, and in the character of its scientific basis, has such intimate relations with these every-day duties of women, is peculiarly adapted as such a means of connection. For what is done or learned by one class of women becomes, by virtue of their common womanhood, the property of all women. It tells upon their thought and action, and modifies their relations to other spheres of life, in a way that the accomplishment of the same work by men would not do. Those women who pursued this life of scientific study and practical activity, so different from woman's domestic and social life and yet so closely connected with it, could not fail to regard these avocations from a fresh stand-point, and to see in a new light the noble possibilities which the position of woman opens to her; and though they may be few in number, they will be enough to form a new element, another channel by which women in general may draw in and apply to their own needs the active life of the age.

We have now briefly considered the most important grounds on which the opening of the profession of medicine to women is an object of value to society in general, and consequently having a claim upon the public for aid in its accomplishment. Let me now state briefly what are the means needed for this purpose.

The first requirement for a good medical education is, that it be practical, i. e., that the actual care of the sick and observation by the bedside should be its foundation. For this reason, it must be given in connection with a hospital. This essential condition is equally required for the more limited training of the nurse, which, though perfectly distinct in character and object from that of the physician, agrees with it in this one point of its practical nature. In Europe, the shortest period of study required for a physician's degree is four years, and at least ten months of each year must be spent in attendance upon the course of instruction. This course comprises not only lectures on the different branches of medicine, but thorough practical study of chemistry, botany, anatomy, etc., in the laboratory, gardens, museums, etc. Attendance on the hospitals is also required, where, for several years, the student is occupied with subordinate medical and surgical duty. This hospital training is the foundation of their education, and the lectures are illustrative of it, not a substitute for it. In England, no medical school can confer a degree that has not attached to it a hospital of as many as one hundred beds. And in many of the best schools, as that of St. Bartholomew's, of London, the college department will only number forty or fifty students, who perform all the assistants' duty of a hospital of five hundred beds, with an out practice of eighty thousand patients annually. In America, though so extensive and thorough an education is not legally required, yet all students who attain any standing in the profession pass through essentially the same course, because nothing short of it will enable them to meet the responsibilities of practice with success.

The chief difficulty in the way of women students at present is, as it always has been, the impossibility of obtaining practical instruction. There is not in America a single hospital or dispensary to which women can gain admittance, except the limited opportunities that have been obtained in connection with the New York Infirmary. This difficulty met us during our own studies, and we were obliged to spend several years in Europe to obtain the facilities we needed. Even there, no provision is made for the admission of women, but there are so many great hospitals in both London and Paris that only those distinctly connected with medical schools are crowded with students. There are many large institutions attended by distinguished physicians, comparatively little frequented by them, and in these a lady, with good introductions, can, if she will give the time and patience, find good opportunities for study.

This troublesome and expensive method is still the only way in which a woman can obtain any thing that deserves to be called a medical education, but it is evidently beyond the means of the majority of women. The instruction that they have hitherto been able to obtain in the few medical schools that have received them has been purely theoretical. It consists simply of courses of lectures, the students being rigorously excluded from the hospitals of the city, which are only open to men. Some three hundred women have attended lectures in these schools, the majority of them being intelligent young women, who would

40

probably have been teachers had they not chosen this profession. They enter the schools with very little knowledge of the amount and kind of preparation necessary, supposing that by spending two or three winters in the prescribed studies they will be qualified to begin practice, and that by gaining experience in practice itself they will gradually work their way to success. It is not until they leave college, and attempt, alone and unaided, the work of practice that they realize how utterly insufficient their education is to enable them to acquire and support the standing of a physician. Most of them, discouraged, having spent all their money, abandon the profession; a few gain a little practical knowledge and struggle into a second-rate position. No judgment can be formed of women as physicians under such circumstances. It would be evidently an injustice to measure their capacity for such occupation by their actual success, when all avenues to the necessary instruction are resolutely closed to them.

Realizing the necessity of basing any system of instruction for women on actual practice, we resolved, seven years ago, to lay the foundation of such an institution as was needed. A number of well-known citizens expressed their approval of the undertaking, and kindly consented to act as trustees. We then took out a charter for a practical school of medicine for women. This plan was founded upon those of European hospital schools. It is as follows: To a hospital, of not less than one hundred beds, lectureships are to be attached, for the different branches of medical science, with clinical teachers to give instruction in the wards. The students should be connected with it for four years, and should serve as assistants in the house, and in out-door practice. Amongst the professorships attached to the hospital should be one of sanitary science, of which the object is to give instruction on the laws of health, and all points of public and private hygiene, so far as science and practical life have taught us with regard to them. This professor should also supervise the sanitary arrangements of the hospital itself, and should be the chief of the system of instruction for nurses. We believe that this professorship would be of real and important value, not only in giving the students a thorough acquaintance with the laws and conditions of health, and fully imbuing them with the idea that it is as much the province of the physician to aid in preventing as in curing disease, but also as affording to teachers and mothers the opportunity of obtaining that sort of knowledge which we have shown they so much need, and yet have no means of acquiring. In this hospital we would also establish a system of instruction for nurses. The plans for this instruction are based upon those drawn up by Miss Nightingale for her proposed nursing school in London,—plans, the result of her long and wide experience, which, unfortunately, her ill health will probably prevent her carrying out, but with which, though never yet published, we are well acquainted.

This is a slight sketch of the mode in which we wish to carry out the three-fold object of the institution, viz., the education of physicians, the training of nurses, and the diffusion of sanitary knowledge amongst women.

It is evident that to organize such a hospital school would be a costly undertaking. It could not be self-supporting, for students are generally barely able to pay for their own direct instruction; and the hospital foundation, the apparatus for teaching, and in the professorships, must be at least in part supported by endowment. It would require, therefore, a very large sum to organize such an institution of the size I have described, and it could not be efficiently carried out on a smaller scale, but could we awaken in the public a conviction of the value of the object, we believe that any amount really needed to accomplish it would be raised.

When we took out our charter we knew that, having few friends to aid in the effort, we must work gradually toward so large an end. We accordingly began the New York Infirmary, as a small dispensary, in a single room, in a poor quarter of the city, open but a few hours during the week, and supported by the contributions of a few friends. Three years ago we had grown sufficiently to take the house now occupied by the institution, No. 64 Bleecker street, and with the same board of trustees and consulting physicians we organized a small house department. This year the number of patients treated by the Infirmary is about three thousand seven hundred. Although the institution is much too small to enable us to organize any thing like a complete system of instruction for students or nurses, we have received into the house some of the elder students from the female medical schools, and a few women who have applied for instruction in nursing. We have thus become more familiar with their needs, and better able to shape the institution toward meeting them.

Although we can not yet realize the ultimate objects toward which we are working, the institution, even of its present size, is of very great value. In the first place, the fact that the entire medical practice of such an institution is performed by women is the best possible proof to the public of the possibility of the practice of women, since, being public in its character, its results are known, as those of private practice can not be. Secondly, it is already a valuable medical centre for women. The practice of a public institution, however small, establishes connexions between those who conduct it and others engaged in various public charities; and from the relations thus formed we have already been able to obtain facilities for students in the city dispensaries, and in private classes, that could not be obtained had we not such a centre to work from. Indeed, so effectual has it proved already in this manner, that were it established on a permanent basis, we could, by its assistance, and our connexions with the profession here and in Europe, enable individual students, possessing the requisite means, to obtain a good medical education before the institution itself can offer the complete education which I have described.

It is, moreover, a charity which is of much value to poor women, as being the only one where they can obtain the aid of women physicians. We have only been able to keep a very small number of beds, but they are constantly occupied by a succession of patients, and we could fill a much larger number if we were able to support them. Our dispensary practice is constantly increasing.

We believe, therefore, that, quite independent of the broader work that may be ultimately accomplished, in its present shape as a charity to poor women, as a proof of women's ability to practice medicine, and as a medical centre for women, this institution is well worthy of support.

What we ask from those who are interested in the objects we have stated is to assist in raising a fund for endowment which shall place the institution on a secure foundation. It has hitherto been supported almost exclusively by the subscriptions of a few friends, who pledged themselves for certain sums during three years. It has been a principle of management distinctly laid down, that the infirmary should not go into debt or on credit; that every year's expenses should be collected in advance, and should never be allowed to exceed the sum in the treasury at its commencement. This rule will be steadily adhered to, and no extension of operations undertaken until the funds are actually collected for that purpose. But so long as we are obliged to collect the income by subscription only from year to year we are not able even to lease a house, or make any arrangement for more than one year, but are obliged to devote to the work of its material support the time and attention that should be given towards organizing and furthering the objects of the institution. New York is the true centre of medical education. One hundred and fifty thousand patients received free medical aid last year; no other city in the Union compares with this in its need of medical charity. It is here, therefore, that a college hospital for women should be established. We have been urged to commence this work in England, and offers of valuable aid have been made for this purpose. But this medical work has originated here, and we believe that it is better suited to the spirit of this than of any other country. As America, therefore, has taken the initiative in this medical reform, let us do the work well.

I said to English friends before I left them, "You must send us over students, and we will educate them in America to do the same work in England." The cordial reply was, "We will send them over if we can not prevail upon you to return to us."

Now, therefore, America must help us to redeem the pledge of education which we have given in her behalf.

Help us to build up a noble institution for women, such an institution as no country has ever yet been blessed with, a national college hospital, in which all parts of the Union shall join. Let it not be a name merely, but a substantial fact, wisely planned and liberally endowed.

Surely this awakening desire of women to do their duty in the world more earnestly, and to overcome, for a great and good end, the immense difficulties which stand in their way, will enlist the sympathy and support of every generous man and woman.

Help us, then, friends! Join the little band of workers that has borne so bravely with us the odium of an unpopular cause. Help us fight this good fight, and achieve the victory, the victory of erecting a noble centre of instruction for women, which shall be not only a glory to the New World, but a blessing to the Old World too!

FOOTNOTES

[1] This lecture was prepared by Drs. Elizabeth and Emily Blackwell, as an exposition of the effort now being made in this city to open the profession of medicine to women. It was delivered in Clinton Hall, on the 2d of December, 1859, and is now published at the request of the trustees of the *New York Infirmary for Women*.

ADDRESS ON THE
MEDICAL EDUCATION OF WOMEN

Prepared by Drs. E. And E. Blackwell.
Read before a meeting held at the New York Infirmary,
December 19th, 1863

The present meeting has been called to consider the subject of organising a Medical College for Women.

I shall take it for granted, therefore, that those present approve of the study of Medicine by Women—either upon the general ground of widening their occupations—or from the feeling that in special departments of medicine, there would be an obvious advantage in being able to consult women—or that they would be valuable as teachers to diffuse sound hygienic knowledge.

There is one other point, however, on which I should like to touch—it is the question of educating good nurses. It has been frequently said to us, "If you would establish a school for nurses,—or if you would make nursing a prominent part in your medical school, it would appeal more forcibly to the public.

Now, we fully acknowledge the need that exists of a good school for nurses. The Infirmary was chartered as a practical school for nurses as well as students; and it has given similar advantages to nurses, in their department, that it has to students—viz., the opportunity of learning, by taking part in practice. In this way it has trained a succession of nurses, who are now employed in New York.

This is a matter on which we have had a good deal of experience. We were engaged in the effort made by the Woman's

47

Central Relief Association at the beginning of the war, to provide nurses for the first military hospitals. Several of our students also have been engaged in these hospitals. Moreover, we are well informed of the results of Miss Nightingale's efforts, both before and since her labors in the Crimea. The result of our experience has been to strengthen our long-entertained conviction, that there must be women physicians to raise up the class of nurses the public require. It is the doctor who must train the nurse; and we have found that men, with the best intentions, find it very difficult to adapt themselves to their instruction; and moreover, that though feeling strongly the necessity, they do not take the same interest in instructing nurses that they do in teaching students. We feel, therefore, that it would be a much easier and more practicable thing to organize good instruction for nurses, after we have formed a medical school, and have drawn together intelligent women, students and assistants, than to form the school for nurses with the hope that the medical school would follow. In fact, we need the higher class to educate the lower, and without them it seems to us impossible to accomplish the work satisfactorily.

We wish it, therefore, to be distinctly understood that a radical improvement in the character and training of nurses, in private service and in connection with public charities, will be the direct result of a superior class of educated women being engaged in medical service—that is of Women Physicians.

Let us then take up the main question, and that we may realize that the practice of medicine by women is a growing influence, and cannot be overlooked, allow me to state a few facts drawn from personal experience.

In 1845 when I resolved to become a physician, six eminent physicians, in different parts of the country were written to, for advice. They all united in dissuading me, stating, "That it was an utter impossibility for a woman to obtain a medical education; that the idea though good in itself, was eccentric and utopian, utterly impracticable!" It was only by long-continued searching through all the colleges of the country, that one was at last found willing to grant admission. When I entered college in 1847, the ladies of the town pronounced the undertaking crazy, or worse, and declared they would die rather than employ a woman as a physician. In 1852, when establishing myself in New York there was the utmost difficulty in finding a boarding-house where the simple name, as physician could be placed; ladies would not reside in a house so marked, and expressed the utmost astonishment that it should be allowed in a respectable establishment. I presented American and foreign testimonials of medical qualification, to one of the city Dispensaries, asking admission as assistant physician, in the department of diseases of women and children; the request was refused. I asked permission to visit in the female wards of one of the city hospitals; the application was laid on the table, not being considered worthy even of notice. There was a blank wall of social and professional antagonism, facing the woman physician, that formed a situation of singular and painful loneliness, leaving her without support, respect, or professional counsel.

Now these few facts taken from individual experience, are fair illustrations of the general feeling of society, and the attitude of the profession towards women physicians in 1852.

Let us see what facts present themselves to justify the assertion, that this new idea is now firmly rooted:

First,—As to the recognition of the propriety of women studying medicine. Since then ten male medical schools have received women as students, and given them the diploma of Doctor. In three states, female medical schools have been established, holding charters granted by the State legislatures; the diploma conferred by them placing their graduates on exactly the same legal footing, as the ordinary physician; the corporators of these female colleges being respectable bodies of men and women, and in some instances enlisting the sanction, by subscription, of a very large number of influential citizens. From the most accurate data, which we have been able to collect, several hundred women have been graduated as physicians at these schools within the last ten years. At five different times, women have been admitted (as exceptions) to our large New-York hospitals to follow the visits of physicians as students, the medical faculties having given their consent in these cases. One of the largest dispensaries in the city, has during the last six years, allowed a little group of respectable female students to continue their daily attendance. The school of Pharmacy has also opened its doors to women as students. No respectable woman practitioner has now any difficulty in holding medical consultation with some of the men most skilled in the various departments of medicine.

These facts will show the growth of professional sentiment, let us see if social feeling has grown in corresponding measure.

Besides the organization of the colleges just alluded to, societies have been formed at different times, for assisting women in the study of medicine; for educating female missionaries in medicine; for popular instruction to women in physiology and hygiene, &c.—these have all come into existence within the last ten years.

I have stated that several hundred women have graduated as physicians within this period; we have traced the history of so many of these physicians, that we think we may truly say, that the majority of them are engaged in active professional life. Some are assistant physicians in the various water-cure and other private establishments, scattered so plentifully through the country; some are employed in large girls' schools, as teachers of physiology, and physicians to the young ladies; some travel from place to place as lecturers on physiological and medical subjects to women, supporting themselves, year after year, in this way; still more are practising as physicians, either alone or in partnership with father or husband. In every part of the Northern and Western States we know of such physicians, who are supporting themselves, and sometimes their families— whose pecuniary receipts vary from a simple living to a handsome income.

Now all will agree that pecuniary success is a very convincing thing! We may deplore the low state of society, which will measure truth by dollars; but nevertheless we cannot shut our eyes to the fact, that the mass of mankind do judge by a low standard. To say, such and such a woman is making $2000 a year by the practice of medicine, creates more respect for the work in the minds of most people, than any amount of argument, or abstract statement of the truth and value of the idea, would do. We can use then this poor, powerful argument of the dollar. We can point out women in Boston, New York, Philadelphia, Cleaveland, and elsewhere, personally known to us who are making more than $1000 or $2000 a year, in a steadily increasing practice; all grown up within ten years!

Several things are proved by this fact. It shows that women can practise medicine in some fashion—they have the head to do it;—that there is nothing in the work itself, to hinder them from doing so—they have the health to do it—; it shows that women will employ them; that imperfect as their education is (as we shall presently see), and with the distinct knowledge on the part of women, that these physicians have not the advantages of education which men enjoy, they nevertheless employ them widely and increasingly.

I think these facts will be considered as establishing the statement that the practice of medicine by women, is no longer a doubtful, but a settled thing; that a new social power is growing up in our midst, concerning which the question is—not shall it exist, but how shall it exist—shall its influence be for good or for harm? It needs but a moment's consideration to see how very deplorable the influence of an ignorant class of female physicians must be!

This brings us to the point to which we wish to call especial attention; the method, viz., by which a thoroughly reliable class of women physicians may be secured.

We will commence the subject by one simple statement—

there is not in the whole extent of our country, a single medical school where women can obtain a good medical education. I trust that no one will construe this statement into an attack upon the schools already organized. We have watched their growth with deep interest; we have been solicited to take part in most of them, and would gladly have done so, could we have conscientiously approved of them; but we are very much in earnest in this matter, and dare not waste whatever influence God has given us; and we think that when we have shown what women really require for a medical education, that all will agree with us that a school is needed, which shall be formed on a different plan, organized on a much broader basis.

Consider how women stand in this matter; how alone, how unsupported; no libraries, museums, hospitals, dispensaries, clinics; no endowments, scholarships, professorships, prizes, to stimulate and reward study; no time-honored institutions and customs, no recognized position; no societies, meetings, and professional companionship; all these things men have, none of them are open to women. One can hardly conceive a more complete isolation.

These are external hindrances; there are still more intimate sources of difficulty. Women have no business habits; their education is desultory in its character; girls are seldom drilled thoroughly in any thing; they are not trained to use their minds any more than their muscles; they seldom apply themselves with a will and a grip to master any subject. It may be said that their domestic duties, nursing younger children, helping their mother in the family, will help them to sympathize with and understand family needs as physicians; this is true, I grant fully the value of such knowledge, and yet it must ever be borne in mind, that medicine is a science as well as an art; it needs knowledge as well as feeling. Let us give all due weight to sympathy, and never dispense with it in the true physician; but it is knowledge, not sympathy which can administer the right medicine; it is observation and comprehension, not sympathy, which will discover the kind of disease; and though warm sympathetic natures, with knowledge, would make the best of all physicians, without sound scientific knowledge, they would be most unreliable and dangerous guides. This want of mental discipline is then a very serious difficulty which women have to contend with in any scientific study, and is an evident and potent reason whey they need, not less, but much more careful training than men, in any such study.

The second difficulty under which women specially labor, is poverty. As a general rule, women are poorer than men, and in addition to this fact of greater relative poverty, it will for a long time, be a relatively poorer class, of women than men who will study medicine. It is the young man of some means, who is apt to enter upon the expensive study of medicine, whose father is able to assist him during the years which must necessarily elapse, before he gains a remunerative practice; but experience has already shown, that they are the young women without means, who endeavour to become physicians. They come from a class notoriously poor, viz teachers; out of nineteen young ladies who have resided in the N. Y. Infirmary as students of medicine, eighteen had been teachers. We have found these students eager to learn; glad to spend any amount of time that might be required to qualify themselves for their new duties; their patient perseverance was admirable—but they had no money—the little fund they had scraped together by saving or borrowing was soon spent and they were compelled to hurry into the practice of medicine, imperfectly prepared, from the impossibility of meeting the expense of longer studies.

I think it will be felt by any one, however little acquainted with medical matters, that for women students, laboring under these numerous disadvantages of position and mental discipline, excluded from existing institutions, unprepared for scientific study, with no pecuniary resources—a medical education complying with the barest terms of legal requisition, and modelled after the very lowest type of male medical education, is entirely insufficient. Yet this is all that is now offered to women. Two short courses of lectures from second rate professors; a little practical anatomy which may or may not be followed; the exhibition of a few cases of sickness, a short and slight examination of acquired knowledge, this is all that is provided. The student receives the honorable and responsible title of "Doctor of Medicine," without having had charge of a single sick person, or attended a single case of midwifery, without even being aware of the immense difference between reading of disease in a book, and detecting and dealing with it under its infinite disguises in the sick room.

Without referring to the important subject of the preliminary education which should be required, there are four points in which a medical college for women should differ from any institution now established for them.

First.—The character of examinations for, and manner of conferring the degree of Doctor of Medicine. 2.—The method of education. 3.—The relation to the Profession. 4.—The necessary foundation for a college.

First then, a change is needed in the character of the examinations, and the manner of conferring the degree which is the seal or stamp of the whole education. The object of examination is to ascertain that the individual presenting herself really possesses the knowledge and capacity necessary for assuming the medical charge of the sick, and the directorship of the health of families. This examination should not be a pretence.

The tests now laid down for women medical students are altogether insufficient. To question twenty pupils, or even one pupil during half an hour or an hour on the substance of a hundred lectures, will very imperfectly ascertain even the theoretical knowledge of the pupil on the one special branch, much less will it show her ability to detect disease and control a sick room. Each pupil should be carefully examined not only in all essential theoretical points in the lecture-room or professor's study, but in the still more vital subjects that can only be tested in the hospital by the sick bed, in the surgical and anatomical rooms, by manipulation and demonstrations, and in the laboratory by familiarity with medicines. Examinations in diagnosis, in the practical applications of every branch of medicine, are essential to judge of the qualifications of a physician. This plan of examinations differs in kind as well as degree, from the system now adopted for women. Of course it is much more troublesome, requires a much larger expenditure of time and thought, but we believe that too much labour cannot be expended on examinations, that they are of the very highest importance in securing a class of reliable women physicians.

Secondly,—The plan of education should be enlarged. This will be evident from the character of the examinations which I have sketched; a student formed by the simple plan of lecturing, could not pass through such examinations. In educating medical students we have to deal with young and comparatively undisciplined minds. An experienced medical teacher (Mr. Paget, of London,) once told me that he considered the age of nineteen as the very best for a medical student to begin his studies. Now the mind at this age, and all undisciplined minds of any age, do not work alone to advantage. There is a natural tendency to acquire information vaguely and imperfectly they need to be stimulated, directed, called to account; they need to be shown how to study. General instruction *en masse* is insufficient, individual instruction is needed; and sub-division into small classes for individual drill should be an essential part of college arrangement for women. The student should be constantly called upon to communicate as well as receive knowledge. The knowledge is not her own until she has used it; and the habit of constantly giving account of what is gained is invaluable in acquiring clearness and precision of thought. In the same way the student must be taught to apply the knowledge gained in the lecture-room, and from books, to the practical duties of the physician. She must be taught how to practice medicine; and the care of the sick under supervision should be an essential part of the future physician's training. (Of course I include in the term medicine, the prevention of disease; the knowledge and application of hygienic law is essential to the education of a woman physician.) This then is the second important change needed in our college system for women; individual discipline, and instruction in practical medicine.

The third point to be spoken of is the attitude assumed towards the Profession. Courtesy and kindly feeling are due to the old and time-honored profession, by those new comers who are still walking with the uncertain steps of inexperience.

It must not be taken for granted that the exclusion of female students from medical colleges and public institutions indicates a settled hostility to the movement. There are many difficulties to be met, in opening to all, facilities which were established with reference to men only, and it should be one great end of special Institutions for women to assist in meeting such difficulties, and forming links with the profession.

Whoever has had experience in this matter will recognise an under current of liberal and generous feeling in the profession, which acknowledges the claim that women have upon their assistance, in any attempt they make to secure for themselves a solid education. Let us then do all we can to deserve confidence, and welcome the interest which is growing in the profession, as they begin to perceive the important character of this work.

Fourthly.—A woman's medical college must be founded on an endowment. Any attempt to commence such a college without means, relying on the fees of students, the self-denial of the teachers, and accidental subscriptions, must result in a very inferior system of instruction.

In undertaking to found a medical college for women, we do not stand in the same position as an ordinary college. The class must necessarily be smaller and poorer. We have not the great incidental assistance which all male colleges have, from the fact that public hospitals and dispensaries are freely at their command. They have the whole influence of the profession to aid them; while the position of a professor or teacher is so much desired, that pecuniary compensation is the least of the advantages connected with it. All this great system of instruction which has gradually been formed for the use of male students is not at present available for women. It is obvious that special arrangements must be made, in order to provide the thorough instruction contemplated for students placed at so great a disadvantage.

This, then, is the last distinctive feature of a good college for women; and these four points, viz., thorough examinations, complete education, friendly relations with the profession, and a substantial foundation, are the improvements which women need, and which the public has a right to demand.

We believe that the time has come to form a really good school of medicine for women. The hospital organization, under the title of the N. Y. Infirmary for Women and Children, has been preparing the way for such a school for nearly ten years, and its working has been watched by the profession even more than by the community during that time. Many of the best men of the medical profession in New York are now prepared to encourage the formation of a medical school for women, in connexion with it. The Trustees of the Infirmary entered into negotiations this spring with the leading medical colleges of New York, to obtain their counsel in this matter. The subject was carefully considered by them; and the result was an expression of friendly interest in the object, with a recommendation to pursue our present plan of action.

We have thus two important elements to start with: an institution of several years' standing, whose directors, whose aims, whose manner of working are already known and approved of; and the friendly confidence of an influential portion of the profession.

Two other things are now wanted, in order to establish a college: money, which men so liberally give; social influence, which women can so effectually exert.

We need such an endowment as will enable us to secure the assistance of first-rate professors, and to commence such a system of education as I have described—thorough, and practical in its character.

It is also necessary that such a body of ladies as well as gentlemen shall join with the Trustees of the Infirmary, as corporators of the College, as will assure the public and the profession, that this effort possesses the sympathy and support of the women of New York.

In appealing to our fellow-citizens for support, or in asking the profession for their aid, it is justly a first consideration with them—is this effort endorsed by the women of our city!

The question has been asked us repeatedly by business men and by physicians.—Can you show that women want this thing done? We know that this question can be answered in the affirmative; we know that there is a wide-spread interest felt by women in this work, and we earnestly appeal to them to prove the truth of this statement by taking part in this effort.

In conclusion we ask all who feel that this is a good work that ought to be accomplished, to realize that it rests with them to assure its success, by an open and decided support.

WRONG AND RIGHT
METHODS OF DEALING
WITH SOCIAL EVIL

AS SHOWN BY ENGLISH
PARLIAMENTARY EVIDENCE

1883

DEDICATION

To all Persons who value Christian Morality as the
Foundation of Permanent National Welfare.

A widespread discussion has already begun throughout the
United States, as to the wisest methods of dealing with social
evil. Much perplexity is felt on this subject, and a feeling of
despondency upon the part of many. A doubt as to the possibility
of dealing with a vast and growing evil in a way that shall satisfy
our highest ideas of morality and religion.   *

In England the subject is attracting an even deeper and more
immediate attention, and certain Parliamentary evidence lately
published in the English Blue Books, throw so much light upon
the subject—show such pitfalls ahead; such failures in one
direction; such cheering success in another, that we can not

do better than study this evidence to aid us in determining the course that we should ourselves pursue.

The following record of facts is laid before women as well as men, because their aid is indispensable for the establishment of sound legislation or wise custom, in all that concerns the relations of the sexes.

In the great majority of the subjects of legislation, the nature and interests of the two sexes are identical; but the fact of natural difference between men and women in one important point, renders it impossible for either sex alone to understand the true aspect of this ineradicable difference, on which just and wise action must be based.

The intelligent aid which is thus demanded from women, can only come from larger knowledge, and earnest study of the actual facts of life. The fundamental error that one sex can govern the several relations of both, is a corrupting fallacy, which has proved destructive of national life in the past. The documentary evidence which follows, shows clearly how all self-styled Christian nations are really drifting to the same destruction which has come upon so many ancient races.

The restraining force of old religious feelings and customs is rapidly disappearing. Up to the early part of this century, when the Roman Catholic and Puritan faiths were still active controlling influences in the life of nations, sexual vice, like other vice, was regarded as an evil thing in men and women; and the efforts made to check it were made on the assumption that it is to be repressed, not accepted. This is seen in the existent Common and Statute Law, i. e. the General Law of the typical nations—France, England, and the United States. But with the gradual decay of religious faiths in the nineteenth century, a change has taken place, and is still going on. English Practice has fallen behind English Law, and the method of dealing with licentiousness has changed in a striking manner.

The Church, also, has loosened its restraining hand. It shrinks from plain and forcible condemnation of this deadliest evil, and neglects to train the young in the strong virtue of purity. In Catholic countries, the Confessional (which, notwithstanding its great inherent evils, did try to deal with this vice) has lost its power over men, and no other institution has taken its place. The Ordinance of Godfathers and Godmothers, which might have wisely replaced the Confessional in the Episcopal Church, is a dead letter. "Discipline" in other religious bodies is relaxed or given up. Thus the difficult but imperative duty of guarding and guiding youth, in relation to their sexual powers, is not provided for.

Religion and Law, equally, must be aroused to the fulfilment of their heavy responsibility toward the rising generation.

53 EAST 20th STREET, NEW YORK,
May 1st, 1883.

I

THE "LET ALONE" SYSTEM

The facts contained in the English Blue Books, to which reference will be made in the following pages, are doubtless familiar to many persons. No apology, however, is needed for again bringing them forward, for it is a duty not to allow them to be forgotten. Some Parliamentary papers of temporary interest may drop out of sight, but these should be kept in view, and urged upon the conscience of every parent in the land; for to the conscientious parent, equally with the statesman, the importance of this evidence can not be exaggerated. A knowledge of facts is the more necessary at the present time, on account of the renewed endeavors to establish a false principle of legislation, which are now being made.

It may not be generally known, that in consequence of the serious facts brought to light in relation to an actual trade in buying and selling young English girls for evil purposes on the Continent, a Select Committee of the House of Lords was appointed in 1881, to examine this subject.[1] The Committee was directed to inquire into the actual facts relating to this traffic, and also to consider whether further legislation can remedy the evil.

Although the work of the Committee was limited to the facts of this infamous traffic, and to the legislation which is necessary to suppress it, the evidence laid before it covers much wider ground. This evidence reveals, both directly and indirectly, facts of the gravest significance in relation to our own condition, as well as to that of our neighbors, in respect to social vice.

It thus renders important assistance toward the solution of weighty but perplexing problems, which are now being widely discussed amongst us.

The great body of facts brought forward in this report, relate to two different but false methods of dealing with vice, methods which have come prominently forward in the present century, in connection with the marked decay of the older forms of religious faith.

The distinctive national tendencies of the French and English nations are strikingly shown in the attitude they have gradually assumed toward the subject of prostitution; the French with their remarkable organizing power tending toward tyranny, the English with their innate love of liberty toward license. These opposite national characteristics, with their results in what may be termed the "let alone" and the "female regulation" systems are here instructively revealed.

The first method to be considered is that of "letting social vice alone" to run its course unchecked. This is the system employed in London.[2]

No systematic and efficient action is taken to check public manifestations of licentiousness. The great Metropolis is not kept in decent order day and night. Solicitation by men and women is not treated as a nuisance in the public thoroughfares, but the streets are allowed to become the assembling places of vicious persons, openly plying a disgraceful trade. Brothels are allowed to flourish, the most abominable acts are left unpunished, and infancy and youth become the prey of every species of corruption.

The facts which reveal the condition of the Metropolis are furnished by unimpeachable witnesses. They are given by such men as Sir James Ingham, the Chief Magistrate of London, a Magistrate of thirty-one years' experience; Mr. Dunlap, Police Superintendent during fifteen years; Mr. Hardman, Chairman of the Surrey County Sessions; Messrs. Arnold and Morgan, Superintendents in the London Police Force, etc., all men of exceptional experience. The following facts are proved by the testimony of these competent witnesses, viz.:

(1.) Coffee-houses and taverns are often used as brothels and assignation places, and registry offices as decoys. See numbers 886, 824, 858, report 1.

(2.) Even the very young are left practically defenceless. They are corrupted in infancy, and vast numbers of children are encouraged in vice by their parents for the sake of gain; 811-15, 579.

(3.) The streets are filled with vicious men and women, native and foreign, plying a vile trade, and tempting the innocent; 152-3, 732-75, 88-96, 915, 12.

(4.) The police are left without instructions, by their superiors, to arrest individuals when they find them actually engaged in the most demoralizing acts; 718, 652-4.

(5.) The magistrates seem often to be without sufficient power (or are not sufficiently stimulated by public opinion) to punish offenders when the offence is a sexual one; 224, 244.

(6.) Brothels are treated as inviolate, except in searching for unlicensed liquor; 230-31.

(7.) At Somerset House certificates of birth are given without hesitation and inquiry, even when it is strongly suspected that they will be used for fraudulent purposes.

The above are some of the chief points brought out by indubitable evidence. They prove the evils and dangers which grow up in all large towns where an energetic public opinion has not begun to restrain the growth of vice.

The most serious danger involved in this state of unchecked evil is the increasingly youthful age of those who are corrupted. A vast and growing number of girls (and boys also) lead a life of youthful corruption. The evidence on this alarming tendency is full and positive. Only a few representative facts given in evidence can here be quoted.

It is stated: "There are houses in many parts of London where people procure children for purposes of prostitution at fourteen, fifteen, and sixteen years of age, without number; the children live at home, but go to the house at a certain hour, with the connivance of the mother, for the profit of the household" (579).

"There is a great deal of juvenile prostitution in my district, quite children, as young as twelve years of age." "The mothers treat it indifferently. I sent for a mother concerning her girl of fifteen; she said, 'I can not help it, she must do as she likes; I had to look after myself at her age, and she must do the same " (717).

Says Mr. Dunlap: "There are a lot of little servant girls about my division, in lodging-houses and other places; they get small wages; they come out on errands and see girls their equals in social standing dressed in silks and satins, while they are slaving; they talk to the girls and are influenced. I have watched the progress of some of these children; they appear with a colored handkerchief over their shoulders, they come two and two through the streets, and after a few days are dressed more elaborately, and at last launch out in silks and satins." "The facilities in the streets are so great that the gentlemen select for themselves" (743 to 46).

A superintendent of fifteen years' standing says: "There has been an increase during my time in the prostitution of very young children. It is a new thing to me. I can not form an opinion as to the cause. This morning, two lads were charged with attempting to steal. A child, not above thirteen, with very short petticoats, her fingers covered with rings, was waiting in the crowd to see 'her man' go down in the van. She found I was trying to get information. She laughed, ran down the passage, and hurried to the Police Court. Most likely she was assisting in keeping 'her man.'"

Says another: "I have been seven years in my district. There are more young prostitutes there than when I first went there. I have noticed during the last six months an increase that I attribute, in a great measure, to a line regiment now lying in the Tower.

The men associate very much with young girls." "At the East End there is a large amount of prostitution of girls, mainly between fifteen and eighteen. They come principally from the large factories. Nearly all the industries of London are represented at the East End. A great many females do factory work, and are prostitutes at the same time, with the tacit understanding and knowledge of their parents. The younger ones take men to low brothels, the elder ones to almost any coffee-house or brothel in the neighborhood. The facilities are very great" (811 to 15).

Says another: "Young girls from twelve, and even eleven, are accosted in the streets by men, who offer money and make improper overtures to them, and so they are led on by the evil associations of other girls, who are older than themselves, to drift into a life of immorality" (865).

Says an experienced Magistrate: "There are assaults committed upon young girls, in many cases by brothers, and even by fathers" (915). "It is an indisputable fact that there are boys and youths soliciting in the streets. The punishment for sodomy is severe; but the difficulty, not to say danger, of obtaining evidence is immense" (652-4).

One of the most experienced witnesses states the following fact: "There is a low description of brothel where the children go. In rooms over a saddler's shop I found two children, certainly not over fifteen, with an elderly gentleman. They laughed and joked me. There were six girls in the house and three men, and the gentlemen were men of mature age" (718).

Let it be noted that the police had no instructions to arrest such moral murderers—men of mature age. There was no one to make a charge against them!

One important fact in this dangerous condition of London must be noted, because it has a direct connection with the system of State-regulated vice, which will next be considered. This fact is the large and increasing number of foreign prostitutes, trained under the foreign regulation system, who resort to London as a free hunting-ground, where men and women can carry on this vile trade unmolested.

Thus it is said: "There are certain districts in London where there are colonies of French prostitutes perfectly well known to the police. The girls brought from foreign countries into this country are generally girls who understand their business perfectly well. They come over here to be professional prostitutes, and they pay the placers to find a house for them" (152-3).

Mr. Dunlap states: "There are large numbers of French and Belgian prostitutes, who use the brothels in the neighborhood" (732).

"Nearly every one of the foreign women has a man living with her, and we have great trouble with the men, who are also foreigners—great, big, hulking fellows, mainly supported by the women. They do not do a day's work; they go to the various cafes and restaurants and wait there to receive the money from the women" (785).

"A few years ago," says the same witness, "a tradesman in the Quadrant assisted the police very vigorously in putting down this vice, and he said it was the *falsest* step he ever made in his life. He has never known what peace or happiness has been since. He is annoyed in every shape and way by the women and the men living with them; these people (men and women) are strong enough to exert pressure upon tradesmen interfering with their vocation."

Such is the condition of London, the British metropolis of four millions of human beings, under the let-alone system; the natural family ties between parent and child destroyed; the streets a public exchange of debauchery for vicious men and women; brothels allowed to flourish and multiply; no check put upon licentiousness; the most abominable acts left unpunished; the police paralyzed; superior officials indifferent or perplexed; and foreign vice and foreign influence making itself more and more strongly felt in that great metropolis!

One noteworthy point comes into view in this evidence, which should be particularly remembered. It is the moral perception and humanity which still exist amongst the English magistrates and police superintendents who give evidence. They have not yet been demoralized by supporting vice. They show an earnest desire to protect the young and check vice. They willingly give their evidence. This book is full of striking testimony to the just and humane tendency of the free and responsible citizen, as contrasted with corrupted and hardened officialism.

FOOTNOTES

[1] See the report of the Select Committee of the House of Lords on the law relating to the protection of young girls. Aug. 25, 1881. Price, 1s. 10d.

[2] It is well to note the fact that the metropolis of Great Britain is not a municipality. The Metropolitan Police are not under municipal direction, and responsible to the citizens of London; they are under the direction of the General Home Office, and under the control of a military officer.

II

THE FEMALE REGULATION SYSTEM

The second method of dealing with sexual evil—revealed to some extent by this evidence—is the Female Regulation System.

This is the plan adopted wherever promiscuous intercourse between the sexes has been distinctly accepted as a necessary part of society.

Under this theory no effort is made to check licentiousness in both sexes, but only to regulate female vice by law, through ordinances framed for the vicious women who take part in such intercourse.

This is the fundamental principle which unites all varieties of the Female Regulation System—whether in its timid commencement in the English Contagious Diseases[1] Act lately adopted, or in the long-tried and logically developed system as we observe it in Brussels. The necessary identity of results, where the same false principle is adopted, will be seen in the facts recorded in the following pages.

Under this system all women of loose or suspicious life are carefully sought for, in order that they may be known to and registered by the police. The purpose of this registration is to bring women under very carefully prepared regulations. On submission to these regulations they may carry on a vicious trade unmolested.

The trade thus carefully ordered and regulated, assumes, in the course of time, all the dimensions of a vast and increasing commerce. Abundant capital is invested in it, talent and ingenuity are exerted to make its resorts attractive and luxurious, and an insatiable demand arises for fresh young articles of commerce.

It is under this system that the infamous trade sprang up which aroused the attention of the British Government.

The evidence in the Blue Book relating to Brussels states that, "Notwithstanding twelve convictions in 1879 and ten convictions in 1880, the brothel-keepers do not hesitate to run the risk of detection and punishment, in view of the material advantage to themselves to be derived from the prostitution of very young girls, who, as inmates of the houses, are more docile, more attractive, more easily deluded, and less exacting than women enrolled for the first time above the age of twenty-one."

The most valuable evidence given as to this foreign system is presented by Mr. Snagge. The weighty character of his evidence is shown by the peculiar nature of his appointment as the special agent of the British Government. Mr. Snagge is an able London barrister, committed to no party or prejudice. This gentleman was chosen and specially appointed by Lord Granville to examine conflicting statements. He was directed to investigate impartially the system in Brussels, and to ascertain the truth or falsehood of the allegations respecting the trade in English girls as connected with that system. Valuable personal evidence is also furnished by members of the Society of Friends, viz.: Mr. Gillet, the esteemed banker, and Mr. Dyer, gentlemen whose names are widely and honorably known.

The chief remarkable difference between the structure of English and of foreign society is the powerful legal organization of female vice which has grown up on the continent.

Mr. Snagge thus describes the manner of life laid down for the girls in licensed brothels by the Brussels municipal authorities. It must be observed that this system, as it grows stronger, always tends to drive women into brothels, on account of the greater ease and efficiency of their management by the police.

"The women in these houses are subjected to obligations without number. They are forced to yield themselves to the first comer, no matter what maybe their repugnance; to incur heavy expenses; to submit to the yoke of the proprietors. They can not show themselves at the doors or windows of the houses; they go out rarely and always under escort; they are entirely subject to the will of the proprietor, and they seize the first opportunity of quitting an existence that affords them so little enjoyment. The result is that brothel-keepers find increasing difficulty in obtaining women. To preserve their popularity with their customers they increase the luxury of their houses, and to procure women they must expend much money."

The theory is that the girls are free to leave, but Mr. Snagge, who visited many houses in company with the officials who have absolute power over them, thus describes the regulations which make the theory entirely false in practice: 1st. The door is always fastened on the inside, the key being kept by the matron. 2d. The girl's own clothes are locked up by the keeper, who furnishes her with clothes which prevent her appearing in the street. 3d. They can only go out with permission of the master or mistress of the house. All these are municipal regulations. 4th. A heavy debt is run up against them—the price paid the procurer being placed on this account—and they are told that the law will not allow them to leave till this is paid. 5th. Those who have been registered under false certificates, which is a penal offence, are held in constant terror of the law. Lastly, they are medically inspected twice a week, and, being always exposed to infection, they spend their time between the brothel, the hospital, and the prison.

The key-note of this whole system is the acceptance through registration of females who, from whatever cause, have begun a life of vice; for registration is the first tentative step taken in the system of female regulation. To this is gradually added the arrangement of minute and stringent regulations respecting residence, dress, behavior, and control of their bodies. As long as they observe the regulations laid down they are unmolested, and are even considered to be fulfilling a necessary and useful function in society.

The idea of wrong-doing is entirely set aside when a prostitute is registered. She becomes by that municipal act an accepted member or trader of the community, and the whole powerful system of accepted and regulated female prostitution follows as a necessary result, as will be seen later.

Besides the organization of licensed brothels, there is an immense number of women living singly in their own apartments (*filles isolées*), erroneously called clandestine prostitutes by M. Treit. They correspond to the women who have been forced into subjection to the English Contagious Diseases Acts. They are registered, inspected, and subjected to police regulations, and protected as long as they observe the police requirements. There are many intermediate steps leading toward the complete Bastiles of vice as seen in Brussels and Paris. The so-called Maisons de Société of Nice, which train giddy, frivolous girls into soulless debauchery, and sell their temporary use to vicious Americans and English for 1,000 francs, are only variations of the same essentially false principle.[2]

Thirdly, there exists an increasing population of poor working-women, whose wages are not sufficient to maintain them, but are eked out by prostitution. This population, in order to preserve its independence, hides from the police, who vainly strive to capture them.

M. Treit, who has been the legal adviser to the British Embassy in Paris for 25 years, gives the following noteworthy evidence of the police system arranged to entrap women. To quote his own words, "If a woman is suspected of prostitution, one or two or three inspectors, under a different dress— times as a workman, sometimes as a gentleman, and sometimes as a servant—follow the young girl for three or four days before keeping her in. If a girl under age is 'taken by a man in the street,' and the mother refuses to interfere, she is registered at the Prefecture of Police." "At this moment clandestine prostitution is very strong in Paris." "Clandestine prostitutes are registered to the Prefect of the

Police." "Every young girl who carries on prostitution must be registered in the Prefecture of the Police, and receive a *carte* with an indication of the medical visit of her home, of her apartment, age, and family."

M. Treit regrets that all female servants in private houses are no longer under police supervision. He remarks, "The regulations (of Paris) are the best that could be adopted. Berlin and all the large towns of France have adopted the regulations of Paris." (See 531 to 556.)

It is very important to note how the full and complete foreign system, as we see it in Brussels and Paris, grows up gradually as a logical necessity from regulating, instead of checking, vice. This method of regulation always begins with timid tentative efforts directed against women. But it grows bolder as it proceeds, and as public sentiment becomes demoralized, until at length a powerful, independent official organization is created, withdrawn from social criticism, and strong enough to resist social reform. Thus we find all officials engaged in administering the system, from the highest Judge, or Minister of State, to the humblest policeman, are henceforth interested in supporting and defending the system against all criticisms or radical change.

The support given on the continent to the organization of debauchery, by the highest Ministers of State, is thus incidentally noted by Mr. Snagge. "M. Bara, the Minister of Justice, a very distinguished statesman and accomplished Minister, desired me to understand that certain institutions existed in their country, licensing prostitution, for instance, which could not be interfered with." (140.)

"The administration of brothels is a very expensive machinery (there are clerks, medical officers, hospitals, dispensaries, and an extensive special police), the municipality derive a profit from the houses," and "the women pay a fee for their registration." (128-143.)

Again, it is stated, "The municipal authority, the Commissaire de Police, even the medical officers, are very lax indeed in the view they take morally of the whole subject; they think it a wholesome and proper institution." "I found out as the result of these trials, that the police functionaries became so accustomed to this system, that they were color-blind to its abuses. Precautions against abuse have no substantial efficacy. The police functionaries favor the brothel-keepers, and wink at a great deal that goes on." (161-2.) Again, "It is within my knowledge from evidence in these trials, that the girls were told by the brothel-keepers, before the inquiry by the Judge d'Instruction, or by the official, that it would be best to say they were very happy. This is a policeman who is going to inquire—'You had better say you are all right; you are very happy, are you not? if not, you had better leave with him.'" (170-177.)

Again, alluding to the great difficulty which we have had in forcing investigation in Belgium, the British Government agent says: "The municipal authorities of Brussels, who had been long accustomed to regulate the Police des Mœurs, were slow to admit evils on the part of their subordinates. In denying the possibility of irregularity or abuse, they appeared to forget that constant contact with the system is apt to dull the moral faculties of officials who supervise it." (App., p. 142.)

This profound remark on the inevitable degradation of the moral sense, when officials are employed to regulate acts of vice instead of to suppress them, is a weighty fact for a Christian nation to recognize.

We see that the Mayor and Magistrates, the Aldermen and Councilmen, even the Cabinet Ministers and ruling classes, become so accustomed to the plan of accepting females for a life of vice, and minutely and carefully arranging their lives, that so far from seeing anything injurious in such a plan, they defend it with energy, and refuse to see the injustice, tyranny, and demoralization which result from it.

This demoralizing tendency of vice, supported by law, is fully borne out by British experience. Wherever immoral legislation is allowed to proceed, unchecked by a death struggle, with an enlightened and vigorous public opinion, resolved to overthrow it, it immediately begins to exhibit the same signs of awful demoralization, cynicism, and cruelty that we observe in Brussels. This fact is painfully established by the contents of a Parliamentary paper, published last August, which will be read by every just and enlightened man and woman with equal indignation and shame.[3]

The British Pro-Consul at Brussels (Mr. Jeffes) states: "The police have been much to blame; the police have been on far too intimate terms with the keepers of these houses." (303.) "The policemen's visits are not useful in protecting the women, as they are always in accord with the keepers."

A Brussels police agent said to an English philanthropist, who urged him to rescue some unfortunate girls: "We can not injure establishments legally authorized, and in which so much capital is invested." Again, "The police, accustomed to consider this traffic as legal, and even licensed and privileged, always encourage and protect it, and especially protect the brothel-keepers."

A striking fact, in comparing the official demoralization which this system produces on the continent, with the British *laissez faire*, is shown in the untruths, the denials, the almost insuperable obstacles which arose in Brussels, when English public opinion began to awake to the fact that an organized and very profitable trade had long been going on to sell young English girls into an obscene imprisonment which has no parallel as yet in England.

English officials in London, and wherever they have not been corrupted by acts regulating vice, although they have often been indifferent to, or ignorant of the course of social evil—see 79, 436, 589, 596—still preserve their moral sense. As has been seen, they willingly give testimony about these evils, and they earnestly make suggestions for their removal. But on the continent there is a mighty system of fully organized government force to support female prostitution; a complete police Bastile banded together to prevent investigation, and to protect a cherished institution. So resolved was this organized force not to be investigated, that the English officials who were first employed to inquire into this trade in girls, were quite deceived. False statistics were presented,[4] damaging facts suppressed or denied, and the English newspaper press was induced to give emphatic denial (based on official statements) of terrible and degrading facts, since proved to be completely true! This is certainly one of the strongest proofs that can be given of the official demoralization produced by regulating instead of suppressing promiscuous intercourse. If it had not been that some upright and patriotic men were privately obtaining proof of these infamous facts, at the very time when the Brussels officials were denying them, and misleading Inspector Greenham (who was first sent over to make inquiries),[5] the English people might never have discovered the extent and dismal character of the infamous slavery to which young girls are condemned abroad. The details of this slavery will not here be dwelt on. It is a slavery in which the municipality clutches the young female body, and uses it henceforth as a machine to be kept in order for the vilest purposes. The horrible facts—which are inevitable results of vice organized by the State—are too revolting to dwell upon. But a debt of gratitude is due to Mr. Snagge from every person and particularly from every woman—for the intelligent honesty with which he has collected these facts; also to Earl Granville for choosing this capable investigator, when a former agent sent over from Scotland Yard had been completely hoodwinked. Leaving, therefore, the hideous details in this Blue Book as a lasting testimony to the social corruption produced by legally regulated prostitution, the statement only will here be given in the calm official language used by Mr. Snagge, of the results of the investigations he was desired by the British Government to make. They are contained in the three following answers:

Answer 1. I find it to be established as a fact beyond all

doubt that for many years a trade or traffic has been carried on, whereby a very large number of English girls—many, if not most of them, under the age of 21 years—have been enlisted to become inmates of brothels in Continental cities in consideration of fees or "commissions" paid by the keepers of the houses to the persons procuring the girls.

Answer 2. I find that fraud was frequently and successfully practiced; that girls under age were easily enrolled; that in the case of English girls, false certificates of birth were the rule rather than the exception, and that the girls entered upon a life, presently to be described, to which they were almost irretrievably committed before they could possibly become aware of its true nature and condition. I find that in several cases, misrepresentation, falsehood, and deceit marked every stage of the procedure from the moment that the girl was first accosted by the *placeur* in England to that of her installation in the maison de débauche.

Answer 3. From the point of view of the "procurers" (*placeur*), young English girls are a form of merchandise to be acquired by industry, and disposed of at a market price per parcel or package. "300 francs par colis" appears to be the ordinary tariff. From the point of view of the brothel-keepers (*tenants maisons*), the girls form a costly portion of their stock-in-trade; they are, like stock upon a farm, kept in good condition, more or less, and prevented from straying or escaping. From the point of view of the girls themselves, they are in some, if not in most instances, following a calling in which they have accepted a life of degrading and dangerous servitude in order to secure the certainty of a livelihood; in other instances they are victims caught in the widespread net of the *placeur*, who has pocketed his fee and decamped, leaving them bewildered and helpless, and abandoned to a fate to which, generally, they become accustomed or inured, but from which, now and then, they are rescued or contrive to escape.

This last answer contains in its few unimpassioned words

the fact which, above all others, must show to every thoughtful person the really diabolical charcter of State-regulated vice. This fact is, the cruelty to ignorant women, the degradation inflicted upon all womanhood, by "accepting" the life of lust as an industry that may be permitted and organized by law.

Mark well the words: "The young girl, thoughtless or fallen, 'accepts' the degrading life to secure a certain livelihood; the innocent girl, deceived and sold, becomes accustomed or inured to this hideous soul-destroying bondage." The innocent girl, as well as the fallen girl, although brought up under the influence of what we call Christian civilization, may thus, under the sanction of State and Municipal laws, accept, and will then become accustomed to, the conversion of her body into a machine for obscenity; whilst her soul, with the connivance—nay, under the sanction—of the State, is allowed to fall into the most hideous depths of our social hell! It is this corrupting influence of the law on the moral sense of womanhood, through the "acceptance" by law of a life of public lust for any woman, which is the most direful and ominous sign of this our nineteenth century of Christianity.

Facts disprove the false and dangerous assertion often made, that if prostitution (*i.e.*, the buying and selling the human body for lust) be restrained and gradually destroyed, no virtuous woman could walk the streets in safety. Exactly the opposite is the truth. It is in towns where the evil trade between men and women is regulated, not checked, that licentiousness grows rampant, and that vice assumes forms of new atrocity. It is in Brussels and Paris that no young woman can walk alone, even in the daytime, without danger of insult.[6] I possess abundant direct personal evidence from women to prove this statement.

Consider a few of the facts which disprove the superficial and thoughtless assertions relating to existing order and safety in Paris.

To understand the full force of these facts, it must be remembered that Paris is much smaller than London; the

Department of the Seine, which corresponds to the Greater London, containing hardly two and a half millions to its four and three-quarter millions, yet the increase of vice, crime, and suicide in Paris is appalling.

"M. Reinach, in the *Political and Literary Review*, lately published, points out that the constant increase in the number of habitual criminals calls for the reestablishment of transportation and the creation of a new penal colony. In Paris alone there are between 20,000 and 25,000 habitual criminals. He dwells with emphasis on the spread of crime amongst the young. In 1879, 18 per cent. of all persons tried in France were minors, being an increase of 3 per cent. in three years. This increase is greatest in Paris, where more than half the persons arrested are minors. Out of 26,475 prosecuted in one year, nearly 15,000 were under twenty-one years of age, the prosecutions including a large number of the gravest crimes. The proportion of juvenile crime has almost doubled in three years."

This month we received the following intelligence from France: "Owing to the insecurity of the Paris streets, as proved by the alarming number of murderous assaults revealed at the correctional police courts, M. Camescasse, the Prefect of Police, has asked that three hundred men be added to his force of *sergents de ville.* Even this increase is considered altogether insufficient under existing circumstances."

"The published statistics of suicides in France during the first three quarters of 1881 exhibit once more that increase in the number of cases which has been observable for several years past—a circumstance the more remarkable since the population has during this period remained almost stationary. In 1878 the number was 6,434; in the past year it is calculated that it will exceed 6,500. In the space of thirty years past the proportionate increase is stated to have been about 78 per cent."

Farther testimony from France gives the clue to the immediate cause of this disruption of society.

"The attention of those suffering from poor wages and only

partial employment has been directed by their leaders toward the luxurious lives of the *bourgeoisie*. There is no doubt that among the less sober and industrious workmen the hatred felt a hundred years ago against the aristocracy is now aimed at that wealthy middle class for which France is remarkable. Madame must have her equipages, Monsieur his mistresses, and the poor suffer."

Again, we have the following statement, written last June, and again and again confirmed: "The state of society in Paris has become very immoral. Obscene literature abounds everywhere, and has led to obscene manners. One of the most repulsive forms of this obscenity is the increase of what are politely called the frail sisterhood, who now infest every quarter, high and low, far and near, to such an extent that from morning to night the streets are encumbered with them. The papers have complained, the inhabitants have petitioned, but to no purpose; somehow or another the Government appears powerless to grapple with the growing evil. It is useless to hide the fact, and whatever squeamish persons may say to the contrary, the truth must be told in plain language. There are things still viler. I allude to their male associates, known as 'les souteneurs' or 'bullies.'"

The increase of this class of vilest criminals—men who live upon women—is inevitable where promiscuous intercourse is regulated, not checked. If rich men buy poor women, leaving them without protection, women will buy poor men to afford them a ruffianly support in the social chaos where they live. We have noted the appearance of this foreign class in London. It has created tumults in Paris, and the unsafe condition of the streets, owing to the increase of ruffians, demands an indefinite increase of the police force.

We dare not dwell upon the atrocious, almost incredible scandals, which leak out in France, notwithstanding the utmost efforts of the police to hush them up. Such crimes as the Bordeaux infamy, the Duphot den of vice, the hideous Fenayron plot, have hitherto been unknown in England. The peculiarity of these atrocities is the astounding sexual corruption which they reveal—a putrefaction of morals, to produce which the element of time is necessary. This complete deprivation of social conscience can only be produced in England through the long-continued and extending influence of immoral law.

When a *law* is made for vice, such law does not confine its influence to the females engaged in the trade; for the law once established, shows henceforth to every person in the nation, old or young, male or female, what attitude is to be taken with regard to the particular subject of the law.

The influence and action of law necessarily extend in logical sequence, from the first timid establishment of a false principle. Thus the State, accepting promiscuous intercourse as a necessity, registers female prostitutes. As a result of this acceptance, the trade must be made healthy, orderly, and ample. As the indiscriminate intercourse of the sexes necessarily produces disease, this, is the first evil which demands attention as sanitary science advances. The first necessary step in regulating the trade in vice, therefore, is to register those who engage in indiscriminate sexual intercourse. But vicious men carry on promiscuous intercourse, and consequently originate and spread disease. Men, however, will not be registered. The State is, therefore, compelled at the outset to leave the most important half of the trade unregulated—that half, namely, that injures the innocent, the unfallen—and that half that supplies all the capital of the trade, the money without which it could not be continued for a week.

The registration of as many females as possible who carry on the trade, is therefore the only possible method practically open to those who, accepting promiscuous intercourse, wish to try and make it healthy. Every result that we have seen in Brussels necessarily follows, from the logical carrying out of this first false step of accepting promiscuous intercourse through registration of women, as a trade recognized by law. Thus, brothels are encouraged on account of their greater convenience of management; and vicious women, living in their own apartments (who are registered), are indulgently treated that they may not hide away.

A chief police functionary of Brussels, who considers these brothels wholesome institutions, says in his report: "It is important that prostitution should, as far as possible, be concentrated in brothels, where superintendence can be easily exercised and scandal hid. They are useful, too, for the discovery of criminals, who frequently resort to them in order to plunge into wild extravagance."

Whilst the moral sense of womanhood is thus corrupted by laws which protect brothels, and raise female prostitution to the rank of an accepted and regulated trade, the degrading effect upon men becomes no less marked. Men refuse to be registered and inspected: they will be free; the State yields, unwillingly it may be, but from necessity, and leaves to men the freedom which rapidly degenerates into license. Unchecked indulgence of the lower nature becomes gradually a demoniac possession. It craves more and more unnatural excitement. The hideous traffic revealed in this Blue Book is one of the direct results of the efforts of mercenary panderers to supply fresh excitement for diseased appetite. It is a weighty fact, which is supported by incontrovertible and most abundant evidence, that vice in both sexes increases far more rapidly, and assumes an intensity of corruption unknown to us, whenever the State accepts, registers, and guards prostitutes, instead of repressing promiscuous intercourse. In such a State, corruption eats into the life of all classes of the community. Licentiousness rapidly increases, and whenever that increases, unnatural and hideous forms of vice increase also. The Authorities, alarmed by the rising flood of corruption, make more and more stringent regulations for women. A band of spies, under various disguises, seek to entrap women. Assignation houses for married women, unknown to their husbands, are established (through M. Lenaars) in Brussels, in order that the police may supervise them. Minor girls are registered in direct violation of the common law of the land. A law to this effect has lately been passed in Brussels, through the instrumentality of M. Bols. These are logical results of the destructive idea that promiscuous intercourse can be rendered healthy by the inspection of every female. Meanwhile, corruption increases to such an appalling extent, that belief in the possibility of purity in men no longer exists in the minds of men or women.

A merchant of Bordeaux thus writes respecting his country: "Sexual immorality is constantly increasing, not only amongst our youth, but even amongst our boys. I vainly seek a remedy for this flood of evil, which will infallibly destroy us, as the Roman Empire was destroyed."

The one true principle of all legal action in reference to sexual vice, with its deadly evils, is now clearly visible to the intelligence of the 19th century; it is this: Male lust must be restrained, in order to check female obscenity. The action and reaction of cause and effect can not be separated. All attempts to do so, result in increasing corruption.

The facts and causes of national demoralization are now plainly before our eyes. Yet so blind are our legislators, our public press, and large numbers of benevolent men and women, to the inevitable moral evil arising from false principle introduced into law, that vast effort is now being made to extend the destructive system of the Continent into our own country.

The imperative duty of ceaseless effort is now laid upon every just and patriotic man and woman, to secure the establishment of righteous law.

FOOTNOTES

[1] See Appendix I.

[2] America will do well to forbid the resort of its naval squadron to the neighborhood of a town which, with its gambling suburb Monaco, has become the most dangerous centre of corruption in Europe.

[3] See Appendix II.

[4] See Note, p. 140 of the Blue Book.

[5] Inspector Greenham 's careful report was proved by subsequent events to be worse than useless. (See Appendix, p. 143.)

[6] See "La Prostitution en France," just published by Dr. Deprès, of Paris, which proves the effect of regulated prostitution in France in exhausting virile energy, and producing violent and unnatural vice through satiety.

III

THE REPRESSIVE SYSTEM,
IN REFERENCE TO MUNICIPAL ACTION

The facts recorded in the foregoing pages prove the dangers arising from letting vice alone; and they also prove to demonstration, the social demoralization resulting from the registration and regulation of the women who take part in promiscuous intercourse.

It is seen that the first system permits great and dangerous evils to run into license, leaving them to be dealt with solely through individual effort, and through the action of the moral and religious organizations, which in a Christian country gradually arise to combat them—organizations indispensable to social progress, but lacking the coherence, force, and educating influence of righteous law.

It is seen also that the last system gradually destroys individual responsibility; little by little it produces cynicism, corruption, and a deep-seated moral degradation in all classes of society, which at last kills the sense of evil in the individual conscience, and thus destroys both the will and the power of a nation to regenerate itself.

It is now necessary to consider in what rightful ways municipal regulation and national law may check disorder and disease, and repress licentiousness in men and women.

These methods will constitute the "Repressive System"—the only righteous method of dealing with vice by means of law.

In reference to municipal action, it is necessary to dwell somewhat at length upon the method employed in Glasgow, because in that city we have proof from actual experience, that all the beneficial results vainly sought for by the Female Regulation System can be obtained without the destruction of social conscience which inevitably follows that corrupt method of organizing female vice.[1]

Glasgow has not yet solved all the problems connected with this vital subject, but it is on the right way to do so. The authorities distinctly recognize that vice in men, as well as in women, must be checked, in any radical method of improvement, and this is the essential point for our century to consider.

The Repressive System, as seen in Glasgow, is the combination of just law, municipal vigilance, and private beneficence, applied to one root of licentiousness. Glasgow is one of the principal British manufacturing towns. It contained in 1881 over half a million of inhabitants. Its size and character will indicate the amount of squalid misery and corruption always found in such a town. The following passage in the evidence shows the astounding condition which formerly existed in this great ship-building and manufacturing town, under the "Let alone" system:

"From twenty to thirty years ago brothels were large places, occupying three or four flats, with a large number of windows, and in the evenings they were all lighted up, the blinds drawn up, so as to attract outward attention, and very frequently you would have seen the inmates lying over the window in a semi-nude state, just to draw the attention of men passing along the streets. It used to be quite a common thing on fine summer afternoons for the keepers of such houses to bring out a squad of women who were living in the house, and parade the principal streets dressed up in their best clothes, and make a circuit round and back to their houses, so as to let it be known where they were to be had."

Mr. McCall, who gives this evidence, has been on the police force for 31 years. All his testimony is given from personal knowledge. In 1870 he was placed in the office of Chief of the police force of Glasgow, a force now numbering 1,069 men. The results of the vigorous administration of existing law during the past eleven years, which he was instructed by the Common Council to carry out, are given in this evidence.

The first and essential step in reform was the growing intelligence of Glasgow public opinion. This opinion demanded more vigorous action. The law was amended by the persistent efforts of the "Repressive Committee" of citizens (to be noted later); and to enforce the law, the police were required to occupy their legitimate position in serving and aiding the citizens.

The necessity of public opinion in directing and supporting the execution of law is constantly referred to in the evidence. Thus, it is said: "Previously to the Act of 1862 the people of Glasgow just thought it (manifestation of vice) was a nuisance that they had to submit to. But, after the provisions of the 1862 Act were more or less exercised, public opinion began to grow, so that it was not regarded as a nuisance that was to be submitted to without something being done to repress it."

Again, it is said, "By 1870, public opinion had matured to such an extent that it was expected that the authorities would do their utmost to repress every brothel, and every manifestation of prostitution that was possible under the Act." (7408 to 10.) Again, it is said, "Public opinion in Glasgow had matured so in 1870, that it would go even beyond the length which the authorities were going in their endeavors to suppress this abomination in the city." Again (7571), "The motive power is the citizen." "It is always a great advantage to have public opinion on your side." (7504 to 6.)

This essential condition of watchful public opinion existing in Glasgow in 1870, when Mr. McCall was placed at the head of the police force, he was required to enforce the existing Act, which, established in '43, and amended in '62, and again in '66, had, from the inertia of the citizens, been allowed to remain, for the most part, as a dead letter.

The law of 1843 enacted "That the owner or lessee of any premises or place of public resort, who shall permit men and women of bad fame, or dissolute boys and girls, to assemble therein, shall forfeit a sum not exceeding £10, to be recovered by summary jurisdiction; that the magistrates may require security for good behavior from such person, and, in case of repeated offence, imprison, eject, or otherwise punish such offender."

A later amendment of the Act confers the following important, but carefully guarded, powers: "Any citizen possessing evidence of the wrongful use of house or premises, may apply to the police, and the magistrate, on complaint of the Procurator-Fiscal, grants a search warrant, lasting thirty days, by means of which an officer of police, *accompanied always by an entirely independent witness*, may at any time enter such place, and carry off persons or things in evidence. The complaint of the citizen must be the first step in the proceedings." (7401).

In Section 7533 it is stated, "It does not matter whether the brothel has been conducted quietly or not, if a citizen, appearing, states to the magistrate that it is a brothel, and a superior official, a superintendent of the police, can corroborate that citizen in his statement,[2] the magistrate is required to issue a warrant, and that warrant extends for thirty days; and, if the police at any time during that thirty days find men and women in the house for the purpose of prostitution, they take into custody the person in charge of the house, the woman who may be the proprietress of the brothel, or any one that she may have managing it for her." Magistrates may inflict fine or imprisonment, and a second time may close the house. But this has never yet been necessary. The people wind it up of themselves. (7570-71.) "The motive power in applying for a warrant must be the citizen. The motive power must always be independent of the police."

By another section of the Act public solicitation is made illegal: "Every prostitute or street-walker[3] loitering in any road, street, court, or common stair, or importuning passengers for the purpose of prostitution shall be liable to a fine of 10*s*. or 14 days' imprisonment." The powers thus conferred to suppress brothels, and to maintain order and decency in the streets, violate no constitutional rights, and leave the police force responsible to the municipality. The police in Glasgow are not a foreign body, imposed by some distant power, and irresponsible to the authorities of the town. The police wear their uniform; they are not disguised in plain clothes as spies upon the inhabitants. Again, the police are required to join the support of the respectable citizen to their own action, whenever they are obliged to perform exceptional acts.

Since 1870 these powers have been vigorously used. Mr. McCall states: "I have held out every facility that the Act affords to the citizens to make a complaint to the Magistrates under the provisions of the Act, so as to suppress those places; and so far as the police, again, are concerned, they have received very strict instructions from myself, that they were to do their utmost to repress this street prostitution, and both those branches have been carried out vigorously."

Two important institutions of Glasgow must here be noted, because they have contributed largely to the very remarkable success which will now be shown to have attended the action of the Glasgow authorities. These two institutions are: 1st, the Magdalen Homes; 2d, the special hospital provision which is freely made for the sick. These institutions were created, and are maintained by private beneficence of entirely spontaneous and independent character, and they are indispensable to any wise repression of these formidable evils.

The large Magdalen Institution has long existed in Glasgow; it has homes connected with it. Into this institution any fallen woman not diseased may enter. There is a very important Committee connected with this institution, called the Repressive Committee. To the initiative of this Committee, which contained several able lawyers, much of the judicious action in Glasgow may be traced. The business of this Committee, besides the special work of rescue, includes the important function of seeing that the authorities are doing their duty in suppressing street solicitation and brothels. (7472.)

The other old institution of Glasgow is the hospital provision, which never refuses free medical aid to any applicant. If any woman, applying for admission to the Homes, requires special medical treatment, she is advised to go to the Hospital, and then return to the Home when cured.

These two large institutions are well supported by voluntary contributions. They are quite independent of the police, but working in harmony with them.

The Glasgow administration—which, as we have seen, includes repressive law, municipal vigilance, and organized beneficence—has been carried on since 1870. Its results may be noted under the seven following heads:

First.—The streets have been cleared of the disreputable business of solicitation and assignation, and left free for their legitimate use as safe and decent thoroughfares.

Second.—The number of brothels has been steadily and largely decreased, notwithstanding the growing population.

Third.—Clandestine prostitution, judging from the most careful observation possible, has decreased generally in the same ratio as the brothels.

Fourth.—There has been a slight decrease in illegitimacy.

Fifth.—An increased desire to reform has been shown by fallen women.

Sixth.—Crime, always connected with vice, has diminished.

Seventh.—Disease, which arises from promiscuous intercourse, has decreased.

Mr. McCall's evidence as to these excellent results is confirmed by a variety of entirely independent evidence. There are not only the series of police reports and criminal returns for the city of Glasgow presented every year to the Lord Provost, the Magistrates, and the Town Council, but there are also the tables of the Registrar-General. There are also the annual reports of the Lock Hospital, and also those of the Magdalen Homes, the reports of these two independent institutions being annually submitted to the city authorities.

It is of the highest importance to note the evidence under these seven heads. Thus, in relation to the condition of the streets, it is said (7413): "This moral clearance of the streets has diminished the number of thefts from the person; but more important than the preservation of property, it has, by removing seductive temptations, saved the young and thoughtless of both sexes from straying from the paths of virtue, and preserved the happiness of many a home" (7405).

"Order and decency are maintained in the streets." (7407). "You may now go along the streets without any interruption."

The facts in relation to brothels, and the effect of law and public opinion upon them, is noteworthy. In 1849, with a population of 314,000, and an inert public opinion, there were 211 brothels, with 538 inmates. In 1870, with a population of 510,816, and a public opinion gradually awakening to the evil, there were 204 brothels. After nine years of vigorous measures required by the citizens, the brothels were reduced to less than one-seventh of the original number. This remarkable result shows the power of public opinion when it demands and supports the enforcement of law.

The great and mischievous error, that vigorous repression of the public manifestations of vice is necessarily productive of an increase of secret vice, is entirely disproved by carefully recorded facts in the municipal experience of this great city of Glasgow.

In his answers to questions (7644-5) Mr. McCall declares, "It is a matter of fact, not mere conjecture, that the administration has reduced the number of prostitutes not residing in brothels." "I have no doubt that the number in Glasgow has been very much reduced in the ratio that the brothels have been reduced." Again (7537), "I am persuaded, especially as regards young men, that taking away the temptation in the streets lessens the desire to go to these women." Again (7413), "It has been alleged that these women have only been distributed and forced into more private resorts. All my inquiries and observations, however, are opposed to the truth of such a statement." Again (7585), "I have not the slightest doubt in my own mind, as a police officer, that the number of prostitutes in Glasgow and its suburbs has been reduced."

There is abundant testimony from this experienced officer, who, with his little army of 1,069 men, is watching this evil, day and night, that, as the brothel-keepers find it unprofitable to keep up their trade, owing to the frequent interference of the authorities, so other branches of this vile trade are also diminishing, under the action of public opinion enforcing law.

This police evidence is supported by the formally-stated and quite independent report of benevolent institutions. Thus the managers of the Magdalen Institution and its connected homes, state: "The Homes during the past year have been kept full, mainly owing to the wholesome enforcement of the Police Act against street solicitation and improper houses. This much-needed repressive action on the part of our civic authorities has had the effect of partially protecting the virtuous, and making the practice of vice more difficult, whilst it has led to a desire on the part of many to be delivered from a life of evil" (7413). In proof of this the statistics of the inmates are given. These, which were only 46 in the year 1860, before public opinion had awakened, had risen to 114 in the year 1871. The number has continued to increase in direct ratio to the vigor of the administration, reaching 244 in 1880 (7463). As stated by Mr. McCall, "They find their calling is so hard and so unprofitable now, that they are glad to take refuge in the institution."

It is said, in relation to the women who enter the hospital: "The poor diseased persons it receives and cures are chiefly young, ignorant, almost always friendless, and wretched; and until brought under the influence and affectionate counsels of the matron, have scarcely ever known what it is to have a kind word spoken to, or a kind action done for, them." In examining the reports of the Magdalen Institutions, it is found that a large percentage are placed in situations or restored to friends. In 1879 fifty-one per cent. were thus aided. The reports abound with letters from these grateful girls.

The important subject of venereal disease is successfully met and provided for, as far as fallen women are concerned. Any measures which tend to check promiscuous intercourse are necessarily beneficial, because it is this evil which is the origin and cause of disease.

No woman who is diseased is admitted as a resident of the Magdalen Institution. No compulsion is exercised, but she is advised to enter the Lock Hospital, and afterward return to the Magdalen. The proportion of women whom the Magdalen has been obliged to recommend to the Lock Hospital has grown less. In 1872, 34.7 per cent. were sent to hospital. In 1880 the percentage had fallen to 18.03, showing the diminution in disease. This is confirmed by the annual reports of the Lock Hospital during the past ten years, which repeatedly refer to the abatement in disease, caused in part by the energetic action of the local authorities in enforcement of the laws for the repression of vice.

In 1875 the gratifying result is presented of 414 patients dismissed as cured, out of 446 under treatment, with the remark, "The medical officers, from careful observation of the character of the disease, arrive at the conclusion that its virulence has been diminished" (7558). In 1878 the medical officer reports: "In reference to the period during which each patient remains under treatment, and the beneficial influence on the public health, the period of residence has been gradually diminishing; the disease is decidedly less virulent in its character than formerly, and is not so commonly found amongst the lower and working classes of the population."

The last Hospital Report for 1880 is as follows: "The medical officers append the following statement: Since the year 1805 the objects which the benevolent founder of this institution had in view have been carried out, and the results are that in this large city, with more than half a million of population, the diseases for which this hospital was opened have become milder in their

95

type, altogether less fatal, and more amenable to treatment than formerly, while at the same time its frequency has greatly diminished, and its effects, even upon the better classes of people, are not so often the subject of medical observation. One of the causes is that there is no restriction placed on the admission of patients—no case is refused from want of accommodation. Every encouragement is afforded, and as the patients are seen early, they are more readily cured. They are kindly treated and spoken to, and ample facilities are afforded them of beginning a new life." Acknowledgment is also given in these hospital reports to " the praiseworthy zeal of the magistracy of the city in vigorously applying the law for the repression and suppression of the particular vice from which these diseases spring."

It should be noted here that the authorities of Glasgow are citizen magistrates, directly responsible to the electors; not stipendiary magistrates elected triennially from among the Town Councillors, and thus farther removed from a responsibility to public opinion. Another quite independent proof of the wisdom of just repressive law is found in the Registrar-General's tables of illegitimacy. These show a decrease of such births in Glasgow during this administration. In 1869 the tables show the proportion of illegitimate to legitimate births to be in 1869, 9.7; in 1870, 9.5; in 1871, 9.4. In the last report it had fallen to 8.2, having fallen from 9.7 to 8.2 during the ten years, or the period of active enforcement of law.

The reports showing the relation of crime and vice, and its diminution when active measures are taken to repress vice, are noteworthy, as they afford such a re-markable contrast to the increase of crime which has been shown to exist in Paris under the Female Organization system.

It is stated, " The summary of thefts is instructive of the good which has flowed from the efforts made by the magistrates and police to minimize street prostitution and brothel-keeping in the Municipality. From the years from i860 to 1869 the total number of informations lodged for street thefts, with or without violence, was 5,067, and the value of the property stolen was £24,446 2s. 4d. From 1870 to 1879 the number of informations of thefts was 2,887, and the value of the property stolen was £1 1,508 19s. 4d. Thus also in thefts committed in brothels during the first period informations were 3,804, and property stolen .£16,843 12s. 6d., but during the latter period only 808 informations, with value of property, £3,077 1s. 11 d.

The testimony of this intelligent, honest, and experienced head of police is thus summarized: "Notwithstanding the frequently expressed opinion of well-meaning people, who take, as they state, a philosophical view of prostitution and brothel-keeping, and, from their mode of reasoning, arrive at the conclusion that both are necessary evils, and incapable of being either eradicated or greatly diminished, I consider myself justified in the opinion that the results indicated above, and which have been brought about by a steady and persistent application of the law by the authorities, have been of very great advantage to this community. Viewed from no higher stand-point than that of profit and loss in property, the benefits are apparent and tangible; but when the social and moral advantages are taken into account, the removal of seductive temptations from the youthful and thoughtless, and not infrequently from the intoxicated and foolish adult; the results, though they can not be expressed in figures, are far more precious. While the reduction in the number of brothels has been so considerable, and the streets have been to a great extent cleared of abandoned women who used to frequent them, I am to the present time without one single complaint from a respectable citizen that prostitution has gone into more secret or private channels, or that the repressive measures of the authorities have inflicted the slightest hardship upon any one." (7433-)

The foregoing evidence from the experience of the great city of Glasgow furnishes positive proof that the public manifestations of vice, and the evil results—disease and crime—may be effectually checked by methods which do not destroy the sense of right and wrong, and degrade womanhood.

Every municipality may thus learn the necessary steps to be taken by municipal regulation, and benevolent effort, to raise the moral character of the community.

1. Arouse public opinion to the necessity of checking licentiousness, and see that the authorities enforce the execution of wholesome regulations.[4]
2. Provide free and sufficient medical treatment.
3. Found an active rescue mission.
4. Simplify legal procedure against brothels, so that the conscientious citizen may be encouraged to take the initiative in their suppression; the support of the police being ordered, and a magisterial search warrant granted, whenever necessary.
5. Suppress public solicitation to debauchery by man or woman.

FOOTNOTES

[1] This evidence is found in "Report on the Contagious Diseases Act," July, 1881. Six shillings.

[2] This should not be necessary, though it would usually be convenient. Its being necessary gives to the police a discretionary power to permit the application. The private citizen making the application would, of course, do so on his own responsibility, if it was made maliciously or without probable cause.—W. Shaen.

[3] This term should apply to both sexes, and, as seen in sentences inflicted by the Glasgow Magistrates, it is so applied in practice. The growing sense of justice, when the authorities work in the right direction in checking social vice, is shown by the determination of the Glasgow municipality to obtain the power of arresting men in brothels.

[4] At common law—" Every brothel is a nuisance liable to indictment." "Every brothel-keeper is liable to fine and imprisonment." "Solicitation in the streets is a legal offence in London as much as it is in Glasgow." (W. Shaen.)

IV

THE REPRESSIVE SYSTEM,
IN REFERENCE TO NATIONAL LAW

The foregoing measures provide the necessary-means of checking social vice from the outside.[1]

But the measure which more than any other will attack the sources of evil, and produce radical and permanent improvement, is the protection of the young. This must be the work of National Law. The protection of the young from corruption destroys licentiousness itself. Whenever the young are educated in self-respect, and into the true human strength of virtue, then the unimpaired force of sexual passion remains as a powerful source of individual vigor, until it flows into its legitimate channel of parentage. Then the devastating disease of licentiousness gradually disappears.

The first imperative duty of every community, therefore, is to say, with authoritative command, to the vicious adult, "Hands off our children," and to punish with the utmost severity any corruption of minors.

The obligation of a nation to protect inexperienced youth, necessarily ignorant of the far-reaching effects of individual action, has been widely recognized in past ages by the Common Law of all civilized countries. It is only the modern decline of Christian civilization which violates this dictum of Common Law. According to French and other Continental Common Law, no minor boy or girl, up to the age of twenty-one, can legally consent to his or her own corruption—i.e., the adult who debauches is held responsible, is subject to punishment, and can not plead the consent of the minor as a fact in justification.

Notwithstanding the efforts always made under the Female Regulation System, to evade the Common Law by municipal ordinance, the Common Law exists, and it is owing to its existence that some of the actors in the Brussels and Bordeaux infamies were condemned to punishment.

But in England, at this day, a child of thirteen years old can give legal consent to debauchery. The vicious adult can plead this consent, and escape punishment.

The necessity of bringing in new and efficient force to- compel wise legislation on this weighty subject will be evident from the following facts:

In 1875, a bill was introduced into Parliament to secure legal protection to girls up to the age of fourteen. This bill was cut down in Committee to the age of thirteen, and thus mutilated, was accepted by Parliament. It will be observed that a law which protects up to the age of thirteen, only guards children of twelve years of age. Children thirteen years old are therefore capable of giving legal consent to corruption.

The same mutilation of a Bill called "Assaults on Young Persons Bill," occurred again in 1880, a measure then introduced to protect children until the age of fourteen, being again cut down in Committee to the age of thirteen.

It is of the highest importance, therefore, at the present time, in relation to future action, to understand two points: first, what arguments were used by the representatives—English Members of Parliament—to refuse protection to children up to the age of fourteen, when the Common Law of Continental nations nominally protects them to the age of twenty-one; secondly, in what way was this mutilation of the bill originally introduced, accomplished? The following record of facts and arguments, as seen in Hansard, will show that the thought and active terest of women must join with the efforts of enlightened men in guarding children:

Firstly.—These important bills were not debated in the

House of Commons. They were examined in the privacy of Committees, and run through in an almost empty House. At the passing of the bill of 1880 so little interest was felt in a measure vitally affecting womanhood, viz., the protection of girls—a bill which, if enforced, would strike the most powerful possible blow at licentiousness—that of the 650 gentlemen who compose the House of Commons, only eighty-six were present. The age of protection was lowered from the age of fourteen to thirteen by a majority of only forty-one in this small House, and without debate.

Secondly.—In examining the scanty record of the private Committees in which these bills were mutilated, it is seen that two arguments were used for lowering the age of protection. Let women and men weigh these arguments. The first argument put forth, is the fear that fraudulent representation might trouble men. That is, that if a vicious man commits fornication with a young girl, she may be, or may pretend to be, under the legal age of fourteen and so try to extort hush money from him.

The second argument is this : that as a girl may legally marry at twelve, and as she may actually become a mother at eleven years of age, or under, that therefore she can perfectly understand the consequences of her actions, and should be held legally responsible for consenting to debauchery. That thus marriage and fornication should stand on the same footing in the eye of the law.

These appear to be the only arguments used for lowering the age of protection.

Thus we find the bill for protection to fourteen, introduced April 14, 1875, was lowered on the second reading to the age of thirteen by a vote of 65 to 21. In the House of Lords, June 8th, Lord Coleridge says it is lawful, by the Common Law of England, for a woman to marry at twelve years, and he uses this as an argument for refusing protection against seduction at that age.

The Lords finally reduced the age of protection to twelve years, but the Commons restored it to the age of thirteen.

August 6, 1880. The Assaults on Young Persons Bill was introduced to raise the age of protection from twelve to thirteen.

August 12th, in Committee. Mr. Hastings (Chairman of Quarter Sessions) "trusted that the age of ten would be inserted instead of thirteen." "A child not quite twelve was actually pregnant when she came into the witness-box." "It would be very hard that a charge of this kind should be brought by a girl sufficiently developed in body to become pregnant, and that a man should not be allowed to plead in his own defence, that the act was done with her consent." "Again, a child of eleven had been a prostitute under training of her mother. Was a man to be placed in peril by the evidence of such persons, and prohibited from pleading consent?" "He had had before him a number of cases, in which the children concerned in them were of an exceedingly tender age. In one case a child of six was concerned, and the counsel raised the defence that the child did not resist. He overruled that defence."—(But)—"He was convinced that the limit of age in the bill was fixed too high, and that the age of ten would be quite as high as it ought to be." "His argument was, that if children of eleven or twelve years of age were capable of prostitution, they were capable of understanding the nature of the Act, and it was unreasonable that a man should not be allowed to plead the girl's consent."

Mr. Warton "felt it his duty to support the amendment." He was in favor of even a lower age than that named in the amendment of the Member for East Worcestershire." "He had only obtained one acquittal." "It was scarcely possible to get an acquittal when a little girl was in the witness box. One reason was that there were Societies maintained by bringing charges of this description. He believed that these Societies, under the pretence of protecting women and children, wickedly tampered with medical evidence." "Among the lower classes acts of indecency were very common, and children became familiarized with those acts at a very tender age. He regarded the age of thirteen as much too high."

Such are the arguments used in a Christian nation, by the people's representatives in Parliament, to prevent the protection of the law being given to poor, ignorant, exposed girlhood!

Although the instinct of every affectionate parent will instantly detect the cruel cynicism of the foregoing opinions, yet it is necessary here to point out clearly the false physiology, as well as the destructive morality, on which these arguments are based. First.—The physiological statement that mental capacity corresponds with physical growth is entirely false.[2] The true physiological doctrine is, that precocious physical development hinders moral development.

Consequently, the earlier the physical possibility of becoming a parent in the boy or girl, the more carefully law and education should protect this important parental function from early abuse and ruinous exercise. This moral incapacity, to judge of the results of their own actions in relation to sexual intercourse, is not only true of ignorant little girls of thirteen and fourteen, who sell themselves for the offer of a few shillings or a pretty dress, but such moral incapacity belongs to all youth. From the age of sixteen to eighteen, thoughtless ignorance, or the blind impulse of physical sex, are generally stronger than the intellectual and moral faculties. Youth at that age are quite unable to weigh or comprehend the very grave and powerful reasons which make early debauchery so destructive to a nation. At that age they have not acquired habits of sexual self-control, unless they have been surrounded early by exceptionally wise human influences. Our youth, until the age of eighteen, most imperatively require the guardianship and help of law and custom. It is the most cruel injury that we can do to childhood and youth to allow the vicious adult to trade upon impulsive inexperience; or to suffer corrupt age to plead that ignorant youth tempted it to evil. The physiological plea, urged in opposition to the protection of the young girl, is false, for the physical woman is a moral child, in the great mass of minor girls.

The second argument, viz., that fornicators must be protected from fraud, is equally false. Law is made for the protection of human beings in right-doing, not for the protection of the vicious in wrong-doing. The argument that a fornicator must be protected in his evil-doing against a young girl who offers to lead him astray, is the most cowardly instance of moral obliquity that can well be brought forward.

There are, alas! too many adult women ready to supply the demands of vice, making broad and easy the road for the unmanly fornicator. Such persons require no exceptional protection from the law. But our children we are bound to protect. Christian society is imperatively called on to demand that the young shall be guarded by law—the more defenceless the more carefully guarded—until age and experience give them the power of distinguishing between good and evil.

The future education of the young into respect for their own human bodies, and into mutual reverence, can only be effectually accomplished when the vicious adult is prevented by heavy punishment from corrupting minors—boys equally with girls.

The protection of minors is, therefore, the first and most important of the legitimate functions of law, and the foundation of every radical method of dealing with this tremendous evil.

The efficient protection of minors from the corrupting influence of vicious adults by just and severe law, and the energetic execution of such law, will destroy the chief root of licentiousness. It will prove the true radical method which law should adopt for checking disorder and disease. It is on this central ground that the great fight between, virtue and vice must be fought out. All the forces of evil will rise in opposition to such protection, knowing well that the corruption of youth is the stronghold of vice. But in the defence of their children the mothers of the race must be heard; their right to act in such a cause is indisputable, and when women call on men to support them in this sacred duty of motherhood—the guardianship of the young—men will rally to their aid, and no power of ancient or modern evil custom can withstand their united energy.

The great and urgent need of our civilization is the united action of men and women in the mighty contest with social evil which is now beginning. The conflict will be tremendous ; but this age is full of promise.

A new force has appeared upon the scene of action. Never before in the world's history have women of trained intelligence, large experience, and religious faith, broken through the bonds of hypocrisy, and, in united and increasing numbers, recognized the possibility, and maintained the necessity, of the great permanent law of national progress, viz., the equal purity of men and women. This is the new force born into the world, and it is hailed with joy by all far-sighted and large-hearted men.

A great work is before our Anglo-Saxon race, which leads the van of human progress. The immediate practical step to be taken is organization.

It must always be remembered that the law which introduces a new code of morality into England—teaching women that disease, not vice, is a crime—was made by a Liberal Government; also that this same destructive law was accepted and confirmed by a Conservative Government. To neither of these parties, therefore, can we look for just moral legislation.

But it is not necessary to wait for the granting of the Parliamentary franchise, for England to carry on a strong moral warfare in a practical shape.

In the municipal vote women possess an aid whose power they have not yet realized. It is a power which, if organized into a moral municipal league, would prove more permanently efficient than even the Parliamentary franchise, for the election of councilmen is the first link in the great chain of free government. It is the first step taken in either a right or a wrong direction. It is the education of the municipalities which will ultimately determine the action of the General Government. Free, enlightened, representative municipalities furnish the elements out of which a future wise State must be built up. The future action of the municipalities, therefore, will decide whether the Government of England shall grow into representation of a strong, free, and virtuous nation, or sink into a corrupt, centralized, military despotism.

We now observe that every year the strife of political parties increases in bitterness and unscrupulousness. Every municipal election is determined by party spirit, and candidates are recommended because they are Conservatives or Liberals—not because they are fitted by character and intelligence to govern a town righteously. Even School Board elections are beginning to share in this false issue.

A grand opportunity is now presented to English women. They have the power of rallying to the aid of those noble men who have vainly sought to stem the flood of political passion and prejudice, and there are signs that the opportunity will not be lost. Englishwomen as well as Englishmen are beginning to demand that at the municipal elections the first qualification required from candidates shall be intelligent morality, not political partisanship; that Watch Committees shall be held to their duty; that Town Councils shall be taught that they are responsible for that moral order of towns which is the foundation of permanent material prosperity.

* * * * *

It can not fail to be of service to us here in America, thus carefully to consider the progress of thought and experience in the older world. The same questions that have become of such vital importance in Europe are of equal import with us.

Here, also, it is becoming evident that the "Let alone system" in regard to social evil can not continue. We are being summoned even now to decide whether "Regulation" or "Repression" shall be the course which we, as a nation, shall pursue. The broad, downward path which leadeth to destruction, vitiating the strong and treading underfoot the helpless and the weak, or the steep, up-hill path, which shall lead us to a higher and purer national life,—a path needing courage and vigilance and devotion to pursue, but leading to assured success—the path of Christian morality—of salvation for one and all. Let us take courage by perceiving that the struggle is not a hopeless one. It is as a light shining upon us that an example is even now set before us indicating that vice may be restrained; that a way is open to us consistent with morality and religion.

A right national choice, made now and consistently carried out, will rescue from unspeakable evil thousands of helpless children just coming forward into life, and myriads as yet unborn, and shall save our national life and civilization from that sure and swift destruction that inevitably follows from a wrong decision on a matter of vital import.[3]

thus carefully considering—the Mother land, whose course of thought runs parallel with our own—has taken another step in the right direction. The animated debate in the House of Commons on the 20th of April, leading to the adoption, by an overwhelming majority, of a resolution clearly recognized as the first step toward the abolition of the Regulation Acts, is thought by many to plainly foreshadow their future fate; and the great moral and religious uprising, evinced by the multitude of petitions pouring in from the various religious bodies, from the laboring population, from societies of earnest men and women devoted to Moral Reform, show an intensity of feeling throughout the country which will probably render such measures impossible for the future.

The practical good sense, as well as the moral and religious feeling of England, is arraying itself against immoral legislation. What England casts out with indignation and contempt, America will never stoop to pick up.

Let us not be behindhand, then, in resolutely striving for the extinction of evil by the wiser method of united and vigilant repression, and careful guardianship of the young. Let us feel that we have individually and collectively a duty laid upon us, in regard to this matter. Every child in our midst will be to us a source of danger and disgrace if abandoned to evil, or a bulwark of safety and honor if rightly educated and protected as a wise government should protect the children upon whom its future welfare depends.

FOOTNOTES

[1] The religious, educational, and economic reforms, which can alone destroy the evil relation of the sexes, are not touched upon in this work. Co-operation, in its widest sense, includes the Land Question, and is the true form of practical Christianity.

[2] False physiology which strives to throw the blame of vice upon the Creator, lies at the root of every evil system. This, however, is not the place to call attention to the errors which abound in physiological and medical books owing to imperfect observation of the tacts of human nature.

[3] Even as these words are in press there comes to us the cheering news that England, whose experience we have been

APPENDIX I

The preceding pages have been devoted solely to the consideration of civil laws and regulations. The Contagious Diseases Acts are military acts, designed exclusively for the physical benefit of soldiers and sailors. A full discussion of the conditions of a celibate army, or of the duty of the military authorities toward the women whom they consider it necessary to regulate for its service, would be out of place in the present work. Military law, however, must be sternly rejected outside the camp. Great civil populations such as Plymouth, Southampton, Portsmouth, must be freed from military subjection. Any attempt to impose military regulations upon a civil population will be resisted to the death by any country which values its civil freedom.

All that has been here shown, therefore, is the proof that the principle upon which the timid English acts are based, is the identical principle which, boldly and logically carried out, produces the Brussels system. The only check which prevents the development of the English acts into the Brussels system (a development now loudly called for by a portion of the public press), is the determined opposition of the just, or religious men and women of the nation. Let that opposition cease, and London will become a Brussels or Hong-Kong.

The following analysis will show the error of supposing that there is any moral intention in the English acts.

PRINCIPAL ACT, 1866

Heading.—An Act for the better Prevention of Contagious Diseases at certain naval and military stations.

There are forty-two clauses.

The first fourteen relate to the establishment of hospitals for diseased prostitutes, with the way in which they shall be instituted, and paid for by the Parliamentary grants to the military and naval services.

The next eighteen clauses refer to the compulsory and periodical examination of any woman, sick or well (within a radius of fifteen miles), whom the police believe to be a prostitute. These eighteen clauses refer to the details by which each woman is required to subject herself to examination for one year; the time and place for the examinations; the surgeons to carry them on; the hospital where any one found to be sick shall be detained in legal custody; the punishment and imprisonment of every woman, well or ill, who refuses to be examined.

The next three clauses refer to the various formalities by which a woman may endeavor to prove that she is not a prostitute and be relieved from inspection.

The next six clauses announce penalties for harboring a diseased woman, and the method of serving notices.

The last clause, No. 42, virtually prevents any woman from obtaining redress, if she has been unjustly accused or dealt with by persons under the Acts. Any woman must commence an action within three months, giving one month's notice to defendant (no matter whether she be detained in hospital or prison). She must place sufficient money to defray defendant's costs in court beforehand, and the defendant may always plead in defence, that he intended to execute the provisions of the Act.

The sole object of the Act, in all its provisions for prostitutes, is to keep them healthy. They are in no way interfered with if they show that they are physically healthy, as is the case with the large majority. The only reference to moral or religious instruction is in clause 12, where the chaplain appointed to all State institutions is as usual provided.

It is an axiom in legislation, that a law is false in principle which is open to great abuses, unless excessive care is exercised in its application.

APPENDIX II

Correspondence relating to the working of the
Contagious Diseases Ordinances of the Colony of Hong-Kong.
Price 9d. August, 1881

The correspondence relating to the abuses committed under the Contagious Diseases Acts in Hong- Kong, illustrates as forcibly the demoralization produced on high officials, as on subordinates, when the State undertakes to organize prostitution.

Sir J. Pope Hennessy, Governor of Hong-Kong, shocked at the death of two women, produced by cruelty and immorality exercised under the ordinances, which were forced on the Chinese by Sir Richard MacDonnell in 1868, writes to Earl Carnarvon November, 1877, and the investigations and correspondence continue under Sir Michael Hicks Beach and Lord Kimberley.

It is painful to observe in this correspondence, that blame, not praise, is the tone assumed in the dispatches forwarded by English statesmen, to the humane Governor who is endeavoring to protect poor heathen women subjected to British rule. There is blame for exposing the wrong-doing of the Hong-Kong agents; blame for the publication of intolerable evils; blame for referring to the sale of children; and there is refusal to believe the evidence of residents or natives, if it tells against the Government regulations.

As the Hong-Kong Acts were established for the physical benefit of "Her Majesty's naval and military forces stationed at, or visiting Hong-Kong," Sir Michael Hicks Beach (Colonial),

115

on learning the infamies perpetrated under these Acts, writes, in 1879, to the Lords Commissioners of the Admiralty for advice. He tells them of such evils as employing paid informers to discover prostitutes; seizing marked money in unlicensed houses; illegal practice of arresting, instead of issuing summonses to, inmates of bad houses; the medical examination of women not prostitutes, etc. To this appeal the Lords of the Admiralty reply that "they decline to criticise the Hong-Kong ordinances, but trust the Act will be continued in that Colony, where it has proved of much benefit to Her Majesty's Navy."

The Admiralty being again urged to act, throw the whole matter into the hands of an official working the Acts.

The correspondence continues during 1881. Through the whole of it, not a word is said about restraining men, not a hint of appeal to the manliness of British seamen to show pity, or an English sense of justice as from a superior race, to these poor heathen women. No suggestion of a law to prevent young girls being sold into brothel slavery. No warning that fines must not be imposed upon women whose only way of paying them is to prostitute themselves or sell their children.

Lord Kimberley, in his final instructions for the guidance of the Government of Hong-Kong, sanctions the following principles:

1. The legalization of houses of ill-fame in consideration of fees paid to the Government, naively remarking: "If the word license is thought objectionable, it can be called a certificate of registration".

2. The systematic medical examination of women.

3. A great extension of the Act to poor women, boatwomen, and washerwomen, to be considered as prostitutes. In order to force this corrupt system upon a weak, ignorant race, unable to protect themselves against the crushing domination of a stronger race, the employment of paid informers going about in plain clothes is justified; and marked money may be paid to a woman for prostituting herself, in order that it may be used in

evidence against her.

The words of Lord Kimberley, a statesman and Cabinet Minister of a Liberal Government, are as follows: "The detection of unlicensed houses was a duty cast upon the Registrar-General and the officers of the Department, and the obloquy cast on them for their efforts appears to me not to be entirely merited. The use of plain clothes seems proper and natural; the use of marked money is not necessarily reprehensible. The acceptance of money in consideration of a request for sexual intercourse is evidence of the character of the recipient; and if the detective or informer, after giving the money, leaves the house, its discovery in the possession of the alleged recipient might be given in proof of the charge." (These are the words of an English Cabinet Minister!) Finally: "Men carefully selected for the work should receive sufficient emolument from the funds raised under the ordinance to ensure trustworthy and competent men, who must be looked for in this country if there is any difficulty in finding them in the Colony."

That is, that a system which is proved by long experience in Hong-Kong, and in every country that has adopted it, to demoralize the agents who enforce it, can only be carried out safely. by agents who are not demoralized!

Printed in Great Britain
by Amazon

54175645R00067